ODDITY
ODYSSEY

With Illustrations by Barbara Smullen

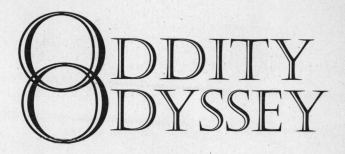

ODDITY ODYSSEY

*A Journey Through
New England's Colorful Past*

JAMES CHENOWETH

AN OWL BOOK
Henry Holt and Company New York

Henry Holt and Company, Inc.
Publishers since 1866
115 West 18th Street
New York, New York 10011

Henry Holt® is a registered trademark of Henry Holt and Company, Inc.

Published in Canada by Fitzhenry & Whiteside Ltd.,
195 Allstate Parkway, Markham, Ontario L3R 4T8.

Library of Congress Cataloging-in-Publication Data
Chenoweth, James.
Oddity odyssey : a journey through New England's colorful past /
James Chenoweth ; with illustrations by Barbara Smullen. — 1st ed.
p.   cm.
"An Owl book."
Includes index.
1. New England—History, Local. 2. New England—Guidebooks.
3. Historic sites—New England—Guidebooks. I. Title.
F4.C48 1996
974—dc20   96-3713
                                                 CIP

ISBN 0-8050-3671-7 (An Owl Book: pbk.)

Henry Holt books are available for special promotions and premiums. For
details contact: Director, Special Markets.

First Edition—1996

Designed by Paula R. Szafranski

1   3   5   7   9   10   8   6   4   2

*This book is dedicated to my wife, Denise,
who has always believed that some day
I would write one.*

CONTENTS

Oddity Odyssey

VERMONT

In 1901 President McKinley walked out onto the bridge connecting the United States and Canada at Niagara Falls. Not wanting to be the first president to leave the United States while in office, he was careful not to go more than halfway across. He need not have worried. George Washington was actually the first U.S. president to set foot on foreign soil. Bet you never heard any politician mention that fact, but it's true. In 1790 President George Washington rode on horseback northward toward what is now Bennington, Vermont. When he crossed the border, Washington entered the Republic of Vermont, which had been an independent republic since 1777 and would remain so until 1791, when it was admitted into the United States. This friendly venture onto foreign soil might seem contrary to his advice about avoiding entangling foreign alliances, but it really wasn't his advice; Thomas Jefferson said it, not George Washington.

It is almost impossible to travel anywhere in Vermont without being reminded of Ethan Allen, his brother Ira, or the "Green Mountain Boys," even though the Allen brothers were born in Connecticut, which is pretty far south of the Vermont border. They adopted Vermont as their battleground before the Revolutionary War as Vermont has since adopted them as its native sons. Of the ninety-one historical markers placed along Vermont highways, fourteen of them (about 15 percent) mention Ethan Allen, Ira Allen, or the Green Mountain Boys, who seem to have been all over the map at one time or another.

Bennington, near the state's southern border, was a prime stamping ground for Ethan Allen and his stalwart lads. Though officially outlaws, the Green Mountain Boys hung around openly at the Catamount Tavern, planning raids on Fort Ticonderoga and Crown Point. They also lay in wait there for upstart New Yorkers who kept invading Vermont under the mistaken belief that it belonged to New York. Intruders were introduced to a "beech seal" flogging—a hearty "chastisement with the twigs of the wilderness." The Catamount Tavern was also where Ethan Allen once faced down an angry lynch mob, though no historical marker mentions the incident.

David Redding may have been a member of the Queen's Loyal Rangers in 1778, but Vermonters figured that was no excuse for his "enemical conduct" in stealing some guns from the house of David Robinson (where they had been stored for safety) and clandestinely delivering them to the British forces. Loyal Brit or traitorous American—it made no difference to the jury which decided to hang him in either case. Then an upstart attorney belatedly pointed out that Redding had been tried before a six-man jury while the law for his crime required a jury of twelve. On the day set for his execution, the council granted a reprieve "until Thursday next."

Unfortunately for Redding, a large crowd had already gathered in anticipation of his execution; they pressed for an immediate lynching. Returning to Bennington at just the right moment, Ethan Allen elbowed through the mob, climbed up on a stump, and shouted, "Attention the whole!" After quieting the riotous mob, Ethan announced the reasons for the reprieve and urged their peaceful departure. He told them to return on the day set for execution. "You shall see somebody hung at all events, for if Redding is not then hung, I will be hung myself."

Determined to carry out his promise (while avoiding his own

demise), Ethan Allen got himself appointed as prosecutor for the second trial. On the ninth of June, in front of a twelve-man jury, Redding was tried again, and Ethan Allen presented his case against the man he had earlier rescued. To the satisfaction of those assembled, Redding was convicted, and two days later was hung in the open field across from the Catamount Tavern. Ethan Allen had been true to his word. And no one mentioned that Redding had been tried twice for the same offence.

David Redding's bones somehow or other wound up in a storage box at the Bennington Museum, remaining for years among bones studied by students in anatomy classes. Sometime around 1976, they were discreetly interred in the Old Bennington Cemetery.

The Catamount Tavern burned down in 1871 and was never rebuilt. The stuffed catamount over its door, meant to warn New Yorkers of the fate awaiting them if they persisted in trying to seize lands in Vermont, went up in flames with the rest. Today the site is marked with a stone monument topped by the statue of a prowling catamount.

Well, it isn't really a catamount. It is the statue of an African lioness that happened to be readily available at the time. The only visible difference between a catamount and a lioness—the tuft at the end of her tail—was promptly amputated with a chisel. Through the miracle of modern surgery, an African lioness became a Vermont catamount. (So much for the tale of a tail.)

Visitors in Bennington should know that the heroic Battle of Bennington (in which New Hampshire patriots under Gen. John Stark successfully defeated General Burgoyne's desperate effort to seize vital supplies in that town) did not really take place in Vermont. Oh, the supplies were there, but the battle was actually fought in New York State, near Walloomsac Heights, several miles west of the site where the 306-foot-tall Bennington Battle Monument thrusts its spire above the skyline today. Every year now on the anniversary date of that battle, Vermont celebrates an official state holiday for an event that really occurred in New York. (It's a very neighborly thing to do, but I sometimes wonder what Ethan Allen would say.)

Ethan Allen is a big man in Vermont history. So is Jim Fisk, another Vermonter, whose impact was on the financial world. Born in North Pownal, a small town near the Massachusetts border below Bennington, Jim Fisk acquired various titles during his life. "Jubilee Jim," the "Prince of Peddlers," the "Improbable Rascal," "Prince Erie," "Colonel Jim," and the "Barnum of Wall Street" are among the more colorful.

A born salesman who began by peddling wares from brightly colored circus wagons, Fisk was soon well known throughout lower Vermont and New Hampshire. The Civil War drew Fisk to Washington, representing a firm in Boston. He did so well selling goods to the Union Army that the Boston firm had to expand, buy more mills, and take Fisk in as a partner. However, his tendency to stack the employee rolls with old friends from Vermont was eventually noted and as the war neared its end, the firm bought out Fisk's interest.

Fisk turned to Wall Street and a working friendship with Jay Gould. Fancy footwork with watered stock and well-timed bribes gave them control of the Erie Railway. In 1869 they attempted to corner the gold market, an exercise in avarice that ended in the Black Friday panic of September 24 and the financial ruin of many a stock market speculator and gambler.

Meanwhile, Fisk's wife Lucy had continued to live in Boston. In her absence, Fisk found himself attracted to a bewitching charmer, Josephine Mansfield, who promptly repaid his devotion and financial support by falling for his good (and greedy) friend Edward Stokes. When the two lovebirds decided to blackmail Fisk with his letters to Josie, Fisk fought back by filing blackmail charges against the pair. They in turn filed suit against Fisk. In time, Stokes's temper came to a boil; he was losing his lawsuit and had been exposed to the world as a contemptible blackmailer. On January 6, 1872, as Fisk was descending the stairway in his hotel, Stokes shot and killed him.

Stokes retained the criminal lawyers Howe and Hummel to defend him. Their reputation for unethical conduct was exceeded only by their courtroom successes. According to a statement made years later by Hummel, agents from their firm discovered there was only one eyewitness to the shooting. They offered that witness a very large sum of money if he would leave the country and never return. He accepted. Stokes was never convicted of the crime that everyone in New York knew he had committed.

Though born in the southwestern corner of Vermont, Fisk is buried across the state in the Prospect Hill Cemetery at Brattleboro. He didn't design his own monument but he probably would have approved. It's a tall marble shaft on a base that has at each corner an attractive woman, immodestly unclothed from the waist up. Each figure represents a particular aspect of Fisk's career—railroads, steamboats, commerce, and the stage. They have no names, but I think of the one holding a large sack of coins as Josie.

Brattleboro has a number of odd claims on Vermont history. On what is now Brattleboro's northern edge, a raiding party of 340 French and Indians stashed their dogs and provision sleds before making a final dash to sack Deerfield, Massachusetts, in February 1704. Fort Dummer, built by the British in 1724 just south of present-day Brattleboro, was meant to protect Massachusetts settlers against further raids sweeping down from the north. It was the first permanent white settlement in Vermont until the hydroelectric power dams across the Connecticut River flooded the Fort Dummer site out of sight to anyone except scuba divers.

On July 1, 1847, the U.S. government began issuing postage stamps, but Brattleboro had been the first in the nation to do so. The Brattleboro Postmaster's Provisional Stamp was issued in 1846. Five hundred were printed; forty-two are known to exist today.

Brattleboro is not all ancient history. For many years it was the home of Estey Organs, a firm that manufactured both small reed and large pipe organs. Beginning in the lumber yard and ending in the studio room, each finished product was played to the satisfaction of the buyer. Estey Organs was world famous. The instruments are no longer being made, but the last factory buildings can still be visited on Birge Street in Brattleboro, the third and final location for Estey Organs.

Fire had destroyed its first two plants. In building this final plant, the owners were determined to reduce the risk of another fire. The method they chose makes these seven large buildings a real oddity. Not only are the roofs covered with fireproof slate, but the walls of every building are sided with slate shingles. Each structure looks as though it is encased in chain mail. Apparently the theory worked. In the only fire taking place there, damage was confined to a single wall.

The oddest event in Brattleboro's history continues to be a puzzle—a mystery that even the creator of Sherlock Holmes failed to solve. It centered on Charles Dickens's unfinished novel *The Mystery of Edwin Drood*. Persuaded by his friend Wilkie Collins to try his hand at writing a mystery story, Dickens began his book, planning to have it published in twelve installments. With only six of them written, Dickens died suddenly in 1870. He left no notes to indicate what he had planned for the unwritten sections.

A year later, young tramp printer Thomas P. James ambled into Brattleboro. A handsome youth with an eye for the ladies, James soon spotted an attractive girl and followed her to her home. With future encounters in mind, James rented a room just across the street. His new landlady was immersed in spiritualism, and for about a year young James attended occasional sittings in her parlor. Without any prior indication that he had been inspired or affected by those sessions, James suddenly informed his landlady that the spirit of Charles Dickens had contacted him and had instructed him to complete the unfinished *Mystery of Edwin Drood*.

Eyewitnesses later testified that on those occasions when Dickens wanted to dictate, James would go to his room, sit in a chair, and fall into a trance. Afterward he furiously wrote down whatever Dickens had dictated to him. Word spread, usually followed by cries of hoax or fraud. But the completed manuscript, which hit the stands less than a year after James began to write, confounded the experts. It was as though Dickens had written the pages himself—or as he would have dictated them for someone else to write down.

Sir Arthur Conan Doyle applied his Sherlock Holmes investigative technique to the curious case. In 1927 he reported that T. P. James evinced no literary talent, either before or after that one manuscript. In fact, James had never written even one paragraph of his own composition before he began writing for Dickens. His education had ended when James was only thirteen, at what would be the fifth grade in the average public school today. Doyle pointed out that the sections written down by James never accentuated or exaggerated the peculiarities of Dickens's original installments, a rare and subtle accomplishment for an expert much less for a poorly educated employee of an American printing shop. Doyle was convinced that what James wrote was not a hoax or a fraud.

Thomas P. James dropped out of sight as quickly as he had appeared. He died in complete obscurity, leaving behind his single legacy—a mystery within a mystery.

Newfane is a great stop after leaving Brattleboro on Route 30 heading north. Most tourists admire the classic architecture of the Windham County Courthouse and the cuisine at the Newfane Inn or the Four Columns Inn. Perhaps a few go there to spot celebrities such as Chevy Chase, Henry Kissinger, John Kenneth Galbraith, or Mick Jagger, all of whom have spent some time enjoying Newfane.

Overlooked by many is the building occupied by the Windham County sheriff. Facing the town green and the courthouse (but at a discreet distance), the existing structure no longer includes a large wing that originally contained twenty-five guest rooms when the building was known as the Windham County Hotel, or, simply, the County House. What made it unique was that while prisoners were incarcerated at one end of the building, any judges, lawyers, witnesses or ordinary transients were housed at the opposite end. Between them was the kitchen where the jail/hotel keeper's wife prepared meals for both groups. (The pass-through for food going from the kitchen to the prisoners is still there, although the prisoners are not. Their former quarters are now used by the county sheriff to store evidence.)

Theodore Roosevelt loved staying in the hotel wing. When he learned that the prisoners received the same excellent food as hotel guests, he remarked, "Someday, when I've got a lot of reading to do and need a rest, I'm coming up here to commit some mild crime." There is no indication he ever did.

On February 22, 1789, a rather unusual marriage ceremony took place in the Field Mansion up on Newfane Hill. During the ceremony the bride, Hannah Ward, was completely naked. The marriage was witnessed by a large gathering. Widowed by the untimely death of her husband, Hannah Ward was burdened by his unpaid debts; under existing law she could not marry again unless her new husband assumed that obligation. Everything she owned (including the clothing she wore or any donated to her before another marriage) was part of her late husband's estate. However, under the same law, if she wore nothing belonging to that estate during the marriage ceremony, her future husband would not be responsible for the unpaid debts.

In the room selected for the wedding, Reverend Taylor stood beside the groom. A far door opened and Hannah Ward, clothed in an old jacket and threadbare dress, entered with her attendants. No veil or train—not even a ribbon in her hair. She removed her jacket and dropped it on the floor. With one attendant, she crossed to an empty closet. They both entered. The door closed. Moments later the attendant reappeared carrying the last of Hannah Ward's garments.

Through a heart-shaped hole in the closet door, Hannah extended her bared arm. The groom clasped her hand and Reverend Taylor began the ceremony. When it was over, new clothing was passed into the closet and an elegantly attired Hannah finally emerged. According to the records, the couple lived happily ever after.

Newfane's major oddity, however, is the site where Sir Isaac Newton rests in peace. A tall marble obelisk behind an iron fence marks his grave in the South Waldboro Road Cemetery a few miles from the center of town. But this is not the grave of *the* Sir Isaac Newton (who died in 1727 and is buried elsewhere)—This is Newfane's *own* Sir Isaac Newton, who was born in 1791 and died in 1864. On the old vital records in Newfane, that was the name recorded at his birth. Nobody seems to know why "Sir Isaac" was selected, but the best guess is that his parents admired the original model. One has to wonder if the playmates of this Newfane model called him "Sir."

As long as you're in the area, Townshend is just a short haul away from Newfane. The Scott Bridge, which crosses the West River at Townshend, boasts of having the longest wooden span of any bridge in Vermont (and a "lattice truss design" that is 166 feet long). To allow for today's heavier vehicles, a concrete pier now provides additional support. The three spans of the bridge stretch to 277 feet. It's Vermont's longest covered bridge and it was the first bridge marked for preservation in Vermont, which, incidentally, has more covered bridges than all the rest of New England put together.

Westward from here is Stratton Mountain, almost four thousand feet high. Today it's a popular ski resort with numerous trails and excellent facilities. During the summer there is a golf academy, horseback riding, and an arts festival. Indoor tennis and swimming are available. All quite civilized.

The west slope of Stratton Mountain is a very different story. Even today it is raw, remote mountain country. Roads from both sides are long and steep, and were even worse in 1840 when fifteen thousand people moved slowly upward along both roads. They rode on horses or in stagecoaches or wagons, or simply trudged along on foot. A stream beside the road provided water. Everything else the travelers needed to camp out for several nights had to be packed in by themselves. Climbing steadily, the long chain of travelers finally gathered at that high point in the pass. When they arrived, there was nothing there—nothing except the man they had come all that distance to hear, Daniel Webster.

Historically, Daniel Webster is New England's favorite statesman. A great constitutional lawyer and a superb orator, he championed the cause of national unity in spite of opposition from his friends. During his debate against Sen. Robert Hayne in the nullification controversy, he spoke his now-famous line, "Liberty and Union, now and forever, one and inseparable!" His skill saved Dartmouth College, twice averted war with Britain, and in the Webster-Ashburton Treaty finally fixed the unfixable problems of our boundary between Maine and Canada. But his popular fame in New England really rested on little causes. He defended a woodchuck. He argued a case involving a horse with a broken leg being dragged through a wall. He used an ax to break down an illegally nailed door.

Disappointed by the failure of his own hope to become president, he was at Stratton in 1840 to campaign for the Whig candidates, William Henry Harrison and John Tyler ("Tippecanoe and Tyler too!"). It was a log cabin and cider campaign. (Webster himself preferred bourbon, as did Harrison.) On the lowest stretch of the western approach was Kelley's Stand, a log cabin "100 feet long from north to south, by 50 feet wide, cut in two width-wise by a drive" for teams to pass through as they went up the road. But there was nothing else except struggle and toil between Kelley's Stand and the top of the pass.

The Whig's "Log Cabin Convention" on Stratton Mountain was held on July 7 and 8, 1840. During those two days, Daniel Webster spoke to the fifteen thousand conventioneers, ate his pork and beans off a shingle, and slept by an open fire. Apparently he never lost his voice.

There are no signs on the road today to indicate where the convention was held, but it can be found easily enough (except in winter, when the road is closed to traffic). A short distance westward from the point where the paved road becomes gravel (or vice versa), a dirt drive appears on the north side. Visible up that drive is a large boulder with a bronze plaque mounted on it. Beyond it lies a neglected picnic spot.

Visitors who stand there wondering how fifteen thousand people managed to crowd together in this vertiginous terrain should not overlook a second boulder on the outer fringe of that clearing. Statues of Webster exist in many halls, cities, memorials, and libraries (including a whistle stop on the Boston & Maine Railroad), but this boulder is the most impressive memento. Carved on it is a bust of Daniel Webster with a tamarack tree behind him and a memorial statement about what occurred there in that remote, all-but-forgotten episode of Vermont history.

Why did the Whigs hold their convention in such a difficult location? One popular explanation is that Webster had been invited to speak at three different sites and so he triangulated the three, selecting this as the central location. In reality, the west slope of the mountain was picked as a midpoint between the two counties that had invited Webster to attend.

To the gathered assemblage, Webster began his speech by saying, "Fellow-citizens, we meet today among the clouds." He was undoubtedly right. But perhaps he was also remembering his younger life, when he had been advised not to enter the field of law because it was already crowded by people with wealth and powerful friends, and Daniel Webster had neither. Now, looking out over the great multitude swarming on the high, steep slopes of the mountain just to hear him speak, he might have recalled his reply at that earlier time: "There's always room at the top."

Anyone bothered by mountain heights might elect to skip Stratton Mountain and head eastward instead. By the side of the road in the small town of Brookline is the only round schoolhouse in America. Built of red brick with five windows and a door evenly spaced around its circular wall, the schoolhouse was designed by a Dr. John Wilson, who showed up in Brookline in 1821, saw the school built to his design in 1823, taught school there during the first term, and then moved on to practice medicine in Newfane.

The real oddity here is Dr. Wilson himself. He was averse to public gatherings and though he could speak knowledgeably about Ireland, Scotland, and the West Indies, he avoided any mention of

Captain Thunderbolt Round Schoolhouse

his own activities in those faraway lands. In the round schoolhouse his desk faced the road, and through the spaced windows, he watched carefully all who passed by.

In the year that Wilson moved to Newfane, the confession of a man named Michael Martin (also known as "Lightfoot") were printed. Convicted of armed robbery, Martin had been hung in Cambridge, Massachusetts, in 1821—the same year that Dr. Wilson appeared in Brookline. Martin's confession covered the activities of himself and his mysterious partner, "Captain Thunderbolt"—two highwaymen who prowled the Irish countryside and the Scottish-English border for almost a decade. With brassbound pistols, they robbed from the rich, gave to the poor, flouted the law, and became the toast of the little people. Obviously well educated, Captain Thunderbolt successfully passed himself off at various times as a lawyer, a doctor, a schoolteacher, or a cleric of the Church of England.

He did not escape unscathed from those episodes. On one occasion Thunderbolt was shot in the calf by a musket ball, which Lightfoot later extracted with a knife. And in another escapade, Thunderbolt's heel was shot off. Pursuit grew hot behind them and they finally split. Lightfoot came to America while Thunderbolt skipped to the West Indies, dropping completely from sight.

When Martin's confession was read in the Newfane area, speculation took note of the similarities in age, height, size, demeanor, and accomplishment between Thunderbolt and Dr. Wilson (including the slight Scottish burr both evinced during speech). What about Dr. Wilson's mysterious sojourn in the West Indies? And didn't he have a slight limp during wet weather and a clumsy foot when he danced? Wasn't he seen throwing copies of Martin's confession into a stove?

Dr. Wilson moved to Brattleboro in 1836. There his marriage failed, as did his practice and his battle with demon rum. Still reticent, he died in 1847. During his final illness, he refused to allow anyone to remove any of his garments, including his shoes and the thick cravat he always wore, knotted high about his neck. But after his death it was discovered that he had a cork heel, a somewhat withered left leg with a round scar on the calf, and a long, ragged scar on the back of his neck. In his house were found English double-barreled guns, brassbound pistols, old swords, and a few heavy gold watches, along with some powder and shot. The cane he usually carried concealed a long stiletto. In truth, it does seem an odd collection for a respectable, law-abiding member of society.

Westminster, upriver from Brattleboro, is Vermont's oldest existing town and the scene of the Westminster Massacre. By March of 1775, King George's courts had pretty much folded throughout the colonies—except for New York, where they still insisted on holding court. And this applied to Vermont, which was considered by them to be part of New York. Colonists living in Vermont had a dissenting opinion.

The New York magistrate decided it was time to hold court in Westminster to hear matters involving the collection of debts. Believing they would not be admitted into the courtroom once the judge arrived, a group of unarmed citizens entered the Westminster courthouse the previous day to be sure their cause would be heard. They had been assured by the judge that no blood would be shed. But while in possession of the building, Tories attacked them.

William French, the first of those who died in the fight, is buried in the cemetery at the top of Court House Hill. A memorial shaft is there as is a copy in slate of the original gravestone where he is interred. They explain that French was shot "by the hands of Cruel Ministereal tools of Georg the 3d.; in the Corthouse, at a 11 a Clock at Night; in the 22d year of his Age."

Dying when he did, a month before the fight at Lexington, William French may have been the first patriot to be killed in the Revolutionary War. He was certainly the first Vermonter. After his death, about five hundred men assembled at Westminster to be sure the judge was taken to prison in Massachusetts. And in January 1777, in the same courthouse where William French was killed, Vermont declared itself to be a free and independent nation.

Oddities continue to make news in Westminster. In September 1994 a Westminster resident was cleaning out the basement of a home he had just bought. He jostled a cigarette-size box the previous owner, an airline pilot, had left behind—and unwittingly set off a two-day search by more than a hundred rescuers for a phantom plane that didn't need help. The box had contained a hair-trigger aircraft distress beacon. All aircraft are required to carry such a device, but pilots are supposed to remove the batteries when the beacon is not actually in a plane. It's a fair bet that in this case the pilot got a nasty letter from somebody.

Westminster is just a short step away from Bellows Falls. Many people there believe the most notorious person in its history was Hetty Green, "the Witch of Wall Street," who became the richest woman in America. Born in 1834, Hetty demonstrated the two sides of her nature as an adult: she was a real genius at making money on Wall Street; she was also a real genius at keeping every cent she made. Hetty inherited money and married wealth (though she made her future husband sign an agreement relinquishing any claim on her money). She confounded masculine Wall Street with her understanding of financial realities. She bought government bonds after the Civil War when other speculators shunned them; Hetty understood that the government would never repudiate its debts. She turned ailing enterprises into profitable ventures.

Hetty was a penny-pinching miser. When she was once charged ten cents for a bottle of medicine, she told the druggist she would bring her own bottle next time and cut the cost in half. Because soap was expensive, she laundered only the lower skirts of her dresses. She carried bits of food in her bag so she would not have to spend money in restaurants. She heated oatmeal for herself on a radiator. When her son injured his kneecap, she tried treating it herself. Failing to cure him, she took him to a charity clinic but was recognized, and payment was demanded. Hetty was outraged. She withdrew her son from the clinic and refused to pay anything. His condition worsened and eventually his leg had to be amputated.

Hetty died because of her miserly attributes. As someone's house guest, she had a virulent argument with their cook about whether money was being squandered to buy whole milk for a recipe when skim milk would do just as well. During the heated debate, Hetty suffered a stroke from which she never recovered. Hetty is buried in the Episcopalian cemetery in Bellows Falls. Some people there will explain that Hetty was a confirmed atheist until she learned that Episcopalians could be buried at no expense, and for that reason she joined the Episcopal Church just before she died. (The legend is not true. Hetty Green was a Quaker. Her husband, an Episcopalian, had been buried in an Episcopalian cemetery, and Hetty joined his church before she died because she had to be of his faith in order to be buried next to him. Perhaps Hetty Green really did love something besides money.)

Unique prehistoric landmarks may still be seen at the base of the cliffs overlooking the river at Bellows Falls. Staring upward are several groups of what appear to be faces carved into the boulders. Many have "horns" or "feathers" protruding from the upper skull that may symbolize them as shamans in Indian culture. This is the only documented prehistoric petroglyph site in Vermont that can still be seen by the curious viewer. But use caution! The edge of the cliff above the carvings is a precarious perch.

The falls themselves are quite impressive. There is a 1781 account (in *The History of Connecticut, by an Englishman*) of an Indian woman in a canoe who was swept into the current above the falls: "Perceiving her danger, she took a bottle of rum she had with her, and drank the whole of it; then lay down in her canoe to meet her destiny." Miraculously she survived and was subsequently asked why she was so imprudent as to drink all that rum while preparing for death. "Yes, it was too much rum to drink at once but I was unwilling to leave a drop of it, so I drank it and, you see, have saved it all."

A certain Capt. Paul Boyton challenged the falls on October 30, 1879. On a pleasure trip down the river, he decided to go through the falls the next morning in his "rubber floating suit." (Unfortunately, there is no record of what this suit looked like.) The water was high and violent. Two thousand people watched as he went into the water and boldly struck out for the center current. He had a difficult time staying in the main stream, eventually disappeared from sight, but later reappeared a long distance downstream. That evening he told his local audience that "nothing would tempt him to repeat the experiences of that day."

For a pleasant ride, follow the Saxtons River westward to Grafton. Grafton is a well-preserved hamlet, courtesy of a foundation that wishes it well. The Middle Town Cemetery is not hard to find. Ebenezer Tinney is buried there—or is he? His gravestone is worth some contemplation. Tinney is buried in a family plot where everyone else is named Tenney. (Seems the person carving his inscription never got honors in spelling.) The last part of Ebenezer's inscription is frequently quoted as being "My glass is rum," but a careful examination of the letters *m* and *n* in the epitaph shows quite clearly that what the engraver intended was "My glass is runn."

Misspellings were probably quite common in those days. Gravestones were slabbed out of quarries and carted around the New England countryside until someone expressed a need for one. An appropriate inscription was hastily (and sometimes inaccurately) engraved. The hourglass on the "Tinney" tombstone makes it quite clear that his "glass had run," not rum. However, small errors seldom discouraged engravers from advertising their wares. The "Tinney" gravestone includes a full confession at the bottom: "Made by A. Wright & A. Burditt, B. Falls AD 1813."

For another oddity, take Route 35 north to Chester. A charming and placid town, it hardly seems a likely locale for the sixteen-year series of more than fifty burglaries that began in September of 1886. Some buildings were burgled more than once; one was broken into six times. The methods used to gain entry were ingenious and risky, and what the burglar took was often bulky and hard to hide—a bicycle, some bundles of shingles, grain sacks from a grist mill. Security for the town rested with the board of selectmen, who did their best. When a reward of five hundred dollars was offered, Selectman Clarence Adams added one hundred dollars from his own pocket. The burglaries continued. A detective imported from Boston got nowhere. The local druggist brought in some guns for nervous townspeople, but before they could all be distributed, the enterprising burglar stole the remainder.

The owner of the local grist mill was puzzled. He kept losing bags of feed and couldn't figure out how the burglar gained entry. Over the years, however, he realized that the burglar favored difficult and ingenious methods. Believing his mill would be targeted again, he selected an upstairs window that could barely be reached even by an agile man. He booby-trapped that window with a shot-gun that would fire if the window was opened. On July 29, 1902, the gun went off. Racing to the scene, witnesses found blood on the windowsill but no burglar. Later that same night, Selectman Adams was found in his buckboard carriage, covered with blood from an injured leg. He claimed to have been waylaid by highwaymen while driving home. Doctors removed eighty-four pieces of number-eight shot from Adams's left leg.

While the town believed its selectman, the local constable had doubts. There were no footprints or scuff marks where Adams said the highwaymen had been standing. Why was the inner side of his left leg wounded rather than the outer side? Why was there no blood on the buckboard seat? The shotgun at the grist mill had fired number-eight shot. Adams's farm was searched and stolen items were found, including sacks of grain from the mill. Charged only with the grist mill burglary, Adams pleaded guilty and was sentenced to serve nine to ten years in the state prison at Windsor. There were no further burglaries. He apparently died there in 1904. Older residents in Chester still talk about Clarence Adams, admitting with some pride that he sure was a scoundrel. The grist mill building still exists as the Grist Mill Gallery, located where Depot Street merges with the Green Mountain Turnpike.

About twelve miles southeast of Rutland is Cuttingsville and the Bowman Mausoleum. It's a well-known oddity, perched on a slight rise right next to Route 103. Easily visible from the road is a larger-than-life figure of a man peering forlornly into the interior of the tomb. He holds a silk hat, gloves, a wreath, and the key to the mausoleum. The statue is that of John Bowman. He is buried inside along with his wife and two daughters. The first daughter died when only four months old. The second died at age twenty-four and Bowman's wife followed her six months later. Bowman was heartbroken. A wealthy man, he erected a $75,000 Grecian temple as a memorial to his family. It took more than 125 sculptors and craftsmen to build it. The 20-foot high tomb, 17 by 24 feet, required 750 tons of granite, 50 tons of marble, and 20,000 bricks. The interior ceilings, wainscoting, candelabra, molded urns, panels, and emblems are enhanced by using plate glass mirrors to produce an illusion of space and depth. There are busts of the three adults and a statue of the baby with arms extended to her mother. Visitors can look through the ornate doorway into the mausoleum.

To reach the oddity at Clarendon Springs, you have to go from Cuttingsville to Clarendon and then on through Chippenhook. In the early and mid-nineteenth century, Clarendon Springs was the oldest and best-known mineral springs spa in Vermont. Asa Smith discovered it in 1776, searching for a spring to restore his ailing health. He drank the water and applied the saturated clay to his painful limbs, and his health improved. He claimed the water had cured his arthritis, rheumatism, and "scrofula." (For the really curious, this last condition is a constitutional disorder of a tuberculous nature, usually characterized by a swelling of lymphatic glands in the neck area and by inflammation of the joints.) Word spread quickly in an age when people would eagerly drink strange water and then brag about its curative value. To house the many visitors before the Civil War, Thomas McLaughlin built the three-story Clarendon Springs Hotel with its long porches and stately columns. Attendance declined after the Civil War, and though the building still exists, it is a slowly fading reminder of its former elegance.

But the water still flows from a pipe connected to the well house, and people still drink it; many of them believe that it promotes fertility. There seems to be some basis for the legend. In the late 1800s a census showed that the eight families living in that vicinity and drinking the water had produced a grand total of 113 children (with only one set of twins), many attending the same school. Perhaps that belief accounted for the popularity of Clarendon Springs and for the endless array of fine ladies in crinoline gowns sitting by the wellhead, sipping "baby water."

Down the road a piece from Clarendon is Wallingford. Nothing there announces to the casual visitor that it was once the home of Col. Matthew Lyon. An Irish runaway, soldier, printer, author, lumber man, manufacturer, miller, inventor, and contractor, he had been prosperous and bankrupt, cashiered and promoted, convicted and then elected to Congress—while in jail in 1798. Matthew Lyon moved into Wallingford in the spring of 1774. He proposed and drilled a militia, was one of the eighty-three soldiers who captured Fort Ticonderoga, and, by 1782, was a colonel with the Green Mountain Boys.

Elected to Congress in 1796, he was involved in the first violent conflict to occur on the floor of the House of Representatives. Taunted by Roger Griswold from Connecticut, he spat in Griswold's face. The next day Griswold attacked him with a cane and Lyon defended himself with some tongs. The House stopped short of expelling him. On July 4, 1798, the Sedition Law was passed, and Lyon was arrested and jailed because of a letter he had written earlier. Friends raised the money necessary to pay his fines and bail him out. It was during this time that he was again elected to Congress. Another arrest had been proposed as he left prison, but he countered with the comment, "I am on my way to Philadelphia." A congressman was immune from arrest while en route to take up his official duties. His vote helped break the tie between Aaron Burr and Thomas Jefferson for the presidency. But apparently there is no memorial to Col. Matthew Lyon in Wallingford.

Head northward beyond Rutland to Pittsford if you want to see an indestructible covered bridge that has really traveled. The Hammond Bridge was built in 1840; its 139-foot length crosses Otter Creek. The flood of 1927 tore the bridge loose and swept it downstream until it snagged, mostly intact. Empty barrels were forced underneath it to float it again. When Hammond Bridge was finally freed, it was towed back to its original position and moored once more. Because the roadway leading to it has been straightened and improved, Hammond Bridge is no longer open to vehicular traffic but can be crossed along its previous route by pedestrians and bicyclists. The bridge is in excellent condition. It can be located seven-tenths of a mile along the road leading west from U.S. 7 to Florence.

Still going north on U.S. 7 from Brandon to Leicester (pro-nounced LESS-ter) you will round a bend and find yourself confronting a huge statue of a gorilla holding a compact car aloft. This curious lawn ornament was created in 1987 by T. J. Neil as an eye-catching advertisement for the car dealership behind it. "Queen

Roadside gorilla

Connie"—a fitting consort for King Kong—is sixteen feet tall, with her uplifted arm adding another three feet. Her bones are reinforcing bars and her flesh is solid concrete, mixed in five-gallon buckets and molded into shape inside encasing mesh. Queen Connie weighs sixteen tons. Her right arm hangs down and children can be photographed sitting on her outstretched palm. At night, floodlights illuminate Queen Connie and the car's lights are on.

A somewhat different monument is prominently displayed in Rochester, a small town east of Leicester on Route 100. A tall, slender marble shaft surmounted by an eagle dominates the center of an otherwise unadorned town common. Erected and dedicated on June 13, 1868, this memorial to soldiers from Rochester was the first such memorial in Vermont. Unlike many other New England towns, the common in Rochester contains only one monument. Oddly enough, it is a battle monument that honors those who died in the Civil War.

What made the Civil War such a tragic memory for this town—a memory unmatched by the deaths of those who perished in other wars? Of the 32,000 soldiers Vermont sent to fight in the Civil War, 153 were from Rochester—10 percent of the town's population. A quarter of that number, forty-one men, were killed—a tragic body count. The names of those who died are inscribed around the base of that solitary memorial in grateful remembrance by a town that grieved early but never forgot.

Middlebury, back on U.S. 7 and above Leicester, has a really rare oddity. Beneath a gravestone in Middlebury's West Cemetery lie the remains of a two-year-old boy who died many centuries ago. Carved on the headstone is: "Ashes of Amun Her Khep Esh Ef aged two years, son of Sen Woset third King of Egypt and his wife Hathor-Hotpe, 1883 B.C." The cross at the top indicates burial in a Christian cemetery. On the upper left is the Egyptian symbol for life and on the right a bird symbol for the soul. Together they mean that the buried prince has entered into eternal life.

How did this happen? Apparently the child's mummy was stolen from its original tomb and sold to Spanish traders. Brought to New York, it was purchased in 1886 by Henry Sheldon, then busy setting up the Sheldon Museum in Middlebury. When the sarcophagus began to deteriorate in New England's climate, the mummy was stored in an attic. Found later in sorry condition, George Mead, chairman of the museum board, believed the mummy should get a decent burial. He had it cremated, dug a hole in his own burial plot, and buried the ashes himself. He then erected a suitable stone over the grave. Fortunately no one asked him to produce a death certificate signed by the last attending physician.

Still farther north is Bristol. A short distance from the center of town, close to the edge of the road, is the Prayer Rock. This immense boulder has a flat surface on which is carved the entire Lord's Prayer. The letters in the inscription are painted white to make them more easily read. The carving was instigated by a Dr.

Joseph Green. Many years ago teamsters and loggers struggled with horses and oxen to haul logs up the steep, muddy slopes behind the rock. Blue profanity often filled the air and young Joseph, working with the woodsmen, took no pleasure in their expressions. Years later, after he became a successful doctor in Buffalo, he paid to have the Lord's Prayer chiseled into the boulder. There's parking space in a small picnic area next to it.

As you get closer to Burlington, Richmond is off to the east, but not far. Those who pass through the center of Richmond frequently stop to stare at what appears to be an upright, almost cylindrical building. The Old Round Church, as it is known, was erected in 1812 and renovated in 1981. It is the earliest American example of a community-type church that is shared by different religions. Four local religious groups decided to build it, for use by each in rotation. The building is actually sixteen-sided, not round. It may have been constructed in this form to take advantage of heat from the sun. Allegedly seventeen men built it, sixteen constructing one side each while the seventeenth added the belfry. Today the church is used for special events, weddings, concerts, and public gatherings.

Not too far away is "Killer Gorge," considered to be the most dangerous river gorge in New England. Local residents prefer to call it Huntington Gorge and are accustomed to inquiries about its location. A sign posted by the gorge warns of its danger and points out that fifteen fatalities have occurred there, including one state trooper who died during a rescue attempt. In reality there have been eighteen deaths since 1950, with nearly two-thirds taking place in the eight years from 1969 to 1976. Thirteen people died while trying to swim in the waters above or below the gorge. Three were rescue attempts, one was an accidental fall from the rocks above the gorge, one was a suicide. (Blasting in 1976 removed a particularly dangerous rock formation, an underwater chute too narrow for humans to pass through.) One-third of the deaths occurred in May, when the water rises higher from the spring melt and college students celebrate the end of the school year. Other deaths took place during high-water times after heavy rains. Fourteen of the victims were male; fifteen victims were under twenty-six years old. At least nine were college students. None of those who died there lived in Richmond, where they learn at an early age not to challenge Killer Gorge.

Jericho, a short distance north of Richmond, lies in the part of Vermont that gets the heaviest and longest-lasting snows. One man there never got tired of snow. "Snowflake" Bentley was born Wilson Alwyn Bentley in 1865. Starting at age fifteen, he spent the rest of his life studying snowflakes.

Capturing a snowflake long enough to study it is no easy task. First Bentley built an unheated shed to use as his workroom. Using a cold, black, velvet-covered board, he would capture a snowflake, rush it to his shed, and carefully transfer it to a chilled glass slide. Holding his breath so as not to warm the slide, he would place it under his microscope and then photograph the snowflake. He eventually collected some fifty-three hundred photographs. A quiet farmer, he never discussed his work with anyone. Reverend Henry Crocker discovered Bentley working in conditions of poverty and wrote a learned article about Bentley's studies. Worldwide recognition eased Bentley's financial burden. In demand as the world's foremost scientific authority on snowflakes, the shy photographer nevertheless remained reluctant to leave his home during winter for fear of missing a snowstorm. He died on Christmas Eve in 1931. A permanent display about Snowflake Bentley can be seen in Jericho's Old Red Mill.

Examining his fifty-three hundred photographs, Bentley concluded that like fingerprints, every flake's pattern is unique and that no two are alike. Other people shared that belief and it became one of our popular truisms. It may not be true, however. In 1988 Nancy C. Knight of the National Center for Atmospheric Research collected and photographed two unusual snowflakes during a research flight over Wausau, Wisconsin. The two snow crystals may not be absolutely identical, but they are certainly alike. For any two things to be absolutely identical, they would have to have been formed at the same moment, otherwise one would be older than the other.

Residents of Saint Albans thought themselves pretty remote from Civil War battlefields. They lived within fifteen miles of the

Canadian border and a full six hundred miles north of the Confederate capital. They hadn't reckoned on the daring scheme of a youthful Confederate raider, Lt. Bennett Young. Raiding came naturally to him. At nineteen he was one of the South's hardest-riding cavalrymen. Captured by Union soldiers in 1863 during an unsuccessful raid, he escaped from a prison near Chicago and made his way to Canada. Convinced that Confederate raids from the north would draw Union soldiers away from the embattled South, he obtained approval to use southern soldiers to rob three banks in Saint Albans.

Discreetly, the small group of twenty raiders drifted into Saint Albans. Some of them lodged in the American House, a red-brick building that still stands at the intersection of Main and Lake streets across from Taylor Park. In the midafternoon of October 19, 1864, the raiders assembled, armed with heavy Colt revolvers and bottles of phosphorus for setting fires. Lieutenant Young stepped into the middle of the street in front of Taylor Park. "I take possession of this town in the name of the Confederate States of America," he shouted—and the raid was on!

It was a comparatively bloodless coup. (The single death from a raider's bullet was apparently accidental.) In one of the three banks being robbed, employees were forced to swear allegiance "to Jeff Davis and the Confederate States of America" before the raiders fled with $83,000 of the bank's assets (leaving behind $50,000 in gold and bonds). Prisoners were herded across the street into Taylor Park and held under guard. The raiders fled northward into Canada with horses seized from local livery stables and with an estimated $200,000 from the banks. Veteran Vermont cavalryman Capt. George Conger led a posse in hot pursuit, but the raiders safely reached Canada with their booty intact.

Hopes that the incident would trigger a border war between the United States and Great Britain dwindled rapidly. Six of the raiders disappeared in Canada. Fourteen were tried on various charges, which were eventually dropped. The Canadian government returned $86,000 in U.S. currency to Saint Albans. Of the twenty Confederate raiders, only one managed to get back to the Confederacy with his loot: William Travis, who wended his way safely south through the entire tier of northern states while disguised as a girl.

The western segment of the Vermont-Canadian border has a troubled history. Two years after Lieutenant Young's raiders crossed it heading south toward Saint Albans, an Irish group called the Fenians gathered in Saint Albans to head north, bent on seizing Canada by force and converting it into an independent Irish republic. An estimated thirty-five thousand Fenians invaded Canada in 1866. After penetrating six miles amid a few skirmishes, they filtered back across the border. Fenian arms were seized by U.S. troops, who arrested the ringleaders for violating neutrality laws and shipped the remaining dejected Fenians southward in special trains.

Close to the Fenian line of march is Enosburg. In a cemetery there lies the body of a woman who was felled by a banana. Anna Hopewell's epitaph is simple, direct, and unadorned.

> *Here lies*
> *the body of our Anna*
> *Done to death by a banana*
> *It wasn't the fruit that*
> *laid her low*
> *but the skin of the thing*
> *that made her go*

Enosburg is where artist David Stromeyer uses his Cold Hollow Iron Works to create and spread enchanting abstract sculptures across six acres of rolling, open meadows for all to enjoy. Seeing these structures for the first time is a bit like watching your first fireworks. Stromeyer has molded steel beams into interlocking shapes and painted them in vivid swirls and arcs of color. For him, "Steel can be fantastically expressive. It can take a bend, a twist, a crunch, a fold, and be left singing its new form forever." Measuring fourteen by fourteen by fourteen feet *Yellow Fin* soars upward like leaping dolphins. Stromeyer has scattered many sculptures across his cleared fields and freely invites us to wander as we wonder.

"Yellow Fin"

What a surprise to find his delightful creations embedded into our traditional New England scene!

The eastern segment of the Vermont-Canadian border lacks the violent history of the western strip. Instead of treating the border as a barrier to hostile penetrations, the people in Derby Line have woven it into the fabric of their daily lives. The Haskell Free Library and Opera House was deliberately built to straddle the border. Construction began in 1901 with the library planned for the first floor and the opera house to occupy the second floor. The entrances to both are on the U.S. side. So is the reading room in the library, but the children's room is partly in both countries and the room containing the books is wholly in Canada, as is the lending desk. Upstairs in the opera house, the stage and a few seats are in Canada while most of the audience is seated in the United States. On both floors an unobtrusive but clearly visible line marks the border.

The building was presented as a memorial gift to the villages of Derby Line, Vermont, and Rock Island, Quebec, with the understanding that it would remain tax free. However, negotiations are continuously under way between the two to adjust separate national requirements about public safety, fire control regulations, insurance, and building maintenance. But the building is over nintey years old and Vermont officials say safety requires some interior changes in the four hundred-seat opera house. Canadian officials say the artwork and architecture there are the historical essence of the building and they cannot be degraded by alterations. So for now the opera house remains silent and empty.

About fifty-five miles south of Derby Line is Groton, Vermont. It was here in 1850 that "Bristol Bill," the notorious bank robber and counterfeiter, was finally captured. He came from Bristol, England, managing to evade capture in many cities there and here until his final arrest in Groton. His last gesture of defiance occurred in the Saint Johnsbury courtroom when he fatally stabbed the prosecuting attorney with a knife during sentencing procedures.

A few miles west of Groton, travelers along Route 302 will come upon a granite monument to William Scott, a Union soldier born on a farm in Groton. After a long and grueling march, Scott volunteered to stand guard duty in place of a sick comrade. Staying awake all night and the following day, he found himself assigned to guard duty for a second night. He accepted his duty without complaint. Toward morning he fell asleep and was discovered by the relief guard. The penalty for sleeping on guard duty was death by firing squad.

Petitions were signed by hundreds of soldiers urging his pardon and sent to President Abraham Lincoln, who then telegraphed a stay of execution. Getting no reply, President Lincoln ordered his carriage and went to the army camp where Scott was to be executed. There he heard the details and granted the pardon. Scott was released and returned to duty.

Scott's subsequent performance as a soldier was outstanding. No assignment was too dangerous or difficult. He was fatally wounded while struggling to save an injured comrade in the battle at Lee's Mill, Virginia. Knowing he was going to die, Scott's final request was that the president be notified about how the "Sleeping Sentinel" had been killed in battle instead of by a firing squad.

An unusually puzzling epitaph can be seen in the cemetery behind the fire station in Plainfield, west of Groton. Mrs. Eunice Page was seventy-three years old when she died in 1888. Her epitaph reads:

> *Five times five years I lived a virgin's life.*
> *Nine times five years I lived a virtuous wife;*
> *Wearied of this mortal life, I rest.*

(What she did during the missing three years remains her secret!)

Just downhill from Plainfield is Barre, known as the granite center of Vermont and possibly the world. The Rock of Ages quarry is the largest in the world. In 1780 the town name was Wildersburgh, but by 1793 residents met to select a new name. The choices narrowed down to Holden and Barre. Debate between the two men contending for their favorite name became so heated that they agreed to a trial by combat to settle the issue. In a barn with a rough-hewn plank floor, they went at it. The Holden champion was stronger. Barre was more agile but wound up flat on his back underneath Holden, who kept pounding him. Squirming around under the blows, Barre counter-punched skillfully and finally wore down his opponent. Barre claimed victory by jumping to his feet and shouting, "There, the name is Barre, by God!" A doctor who witnessed the combat spent most of the next day removing from the victor's back and buttocks the many splinters Barre had picked up while writhing on the rough floor.

South of Barre is Brookfield. In a book about its history, these questions are asked: What goes from bank to bank yet seldom moves and is at times a diving platform, a truck wash, a film star, a swimming instructor, and a shortcut? The answer is the "floating bridge" in Pond Village at Brookfield. It is the only floating bridge in New England. Back in 1810, residents on the west side of the pond found it difficult to reach the community on the east side in the summer (in the winter they could simply cross over on ice). In

1820 a bridge of logs was built on top of the ice, and when the ice melted, the bridge floated. A few years later the residents devised a flotation system using tarred wooden barrels. The seventh floating bridge was built in 1978, this time by the state of Vermont. Plastic containers filled with styrofoam replaced the wooden barrels, and raised sidewalks allowed pedestrians to keep their feet dry while crossing.

Somehow the current version lacks the ambience of the earlier bridges. Older residents of Pond Village recall how college students used to skinny dip off the bridge when classes ended in June. They smile about how one family of boys used to paddle caskets around in the pond, using them as rowboats. An Olympic hopeful practiced sculling on the pond's quiet water. Part of the local fun was watching "summer folk" try to cross over the earlier bridges by tightrope walking along the curb to keep from getting their feet wet. The current bridge doesn't incite such shenanigans. However, it is still the only floating bridge in New England, and the sign urging those using the bridge to beware of trolls under it never got replaced.

Anything else about Vermont? Well, just a few miles northwest of the floating bridge is the one place where you can be sure that Vermont will not tilt under your feet. The exact geographic center of Vermont is located just three miles east of Roxbury. Stand there and enjoy the scenery!

NEW HAMPSHIRE

New Hampshire's border is an oddity in itself. Its total peripheral boundary line is 598 miles long. Inside the eighteen miles of water boundary separating it from Maine are 130 miles of tidal coastline. On the western edge, the Connecticut River divides New Hampshire from Vermont for 235 miles. For what appears to be a land-locked state, New Hampshire has a surprising 365 miles of wet shoreline. That's more than half of its boundary.

When a body of water is used as a boundary marker, the traditional rule of thumb is to divide it down the middle. For example, a Massachusetts lake separating two Indian tribes had a jawbreaker name that is loosely translated as: "You fish on your side, we fish on our side, and nobody fishes in the middle." However, the Connecticut River boundary between Vermont and New Hampshire doesn't quite work that way. Conflicting deeds issued over the years by various authorities cast legal doubts about who owned what and about the exact location of the boundary line between the two states.

The argument finally went to the Supreme Court, which rendered its decision in 1936: the Connecticut River was the sole property of New Hampshire, all the way across to the low water line on the Vermont side. It then became necessary to survey that side of the river and place boundary markers to identify the low water line.

Exactly where should that survey start? With magisterial wisdom, the Court decided it should begin at the "Mud Turtle" monument. It is an odd name for a monument that no one has seen since 1970. Even stranger is the fact that we know exactly where it is. It stands today where it stood in 1936, at the spot where the western edge of the Connecticut River crosses the Massachusetts border. From that monument the boundary line between Vermont and New Hampshire snakes its way northward.

The Mud Turtle monument has been described as a granite pyramid with a copper bolt at its apex. The granite was sunk into a bed of concrete that was then embedded twelve feet deep in the earth. Apparently the Mud Turtle monument got its nickname from the profile it developed as river mud and silt began swirling around it from the moment it was planted in 1895.

What does it look like today? Nobody knows. When dams built for hydroelectric power began impeding the river's flow, the water level slowly rose. Gradually the Mud Turtle monument disappeared. Since then, the submerged terrapin emerged only once, when work was being done on the Turner Dam in the fall of 1969 and the Connecticut River was running low. Completely buried by then, the monument's location was eventually pinpointed and a digging operation began.

The Mud Turtle finally emerged on October 26. It was viewed by curious visitors for a few months, but when work on the new dam was completed in 1970, rising waters slowly covered the Mud Turtle. Now three fathoms deep, the monument continues to be covered by river silt and sediment. Though it may never be seen again, it still does what it was created to do: it anchors the boundary line between New Hampshire and Vermont.

You might think it is impossible to drive into New Hampshire from Vermont without crossing the Connecticut River, and indeed that is the common belief. Oddly enough, however, it can be done. For a distance of about two miles, the northeastern corner of Vermont is overhung by a small segment of New Hampshire. Using

New Hampshire 102, one can pass over that common border in either direction without crossing any water.

Traffic jams are probably rare in that area even though several unusual locations are but a stone's throw from there. At the western end of this short border is the T-junction where it is possible to stand with one foot in Vermont and one in New Hampshire, and, by bending over, leave a hand print in Canada.

Not far from there is Pittsburg, New Hampshire, which has a Main Street thirty miles long. In area it is the largest township in the country. Pittsburg is the somewhat uninspired name for what used to be the Indian Stream Territory, an independent nation created in 1832 when its fifty-nine families voted (fifty-six to three) to have their own constitution, governing assembly, and militia (of forty-one men). Forced by border disputes to join either America or Canada, it reluctantly became part of New Hampshire, bowing to the American argument that unless the republic was part of the United States it could not be defended by the United States.

Dixville Notch appears on television once every four years during the presidential elections. The Dixville Notch polling booths open just after midnight on election day and close right after the town's twenty-four registered voters have cast their ballots. The vote from Dixville Notch is always first in the nation.

Let's face it. This is a rather remote patch on New Hampshire's western border. Most people crossing into it from Vermont do so farther south, where the road east from Brattleboro skirts the town of Keene. Keene's Main Street is 172 feet wide and paved all the way. The town claims that it has the widest paved Main Street in America—though Brunswick, Maine, has a Main Street that is 198 feet wide. What is beyond dispute, however, is that Keene holds the world's record for having the most jack-o-lanterns assembled at one time in a single place. Carved by Keene citizens in 1993 for their annual Harvest Festival, 4,817 pumpkins were lined up on special scaffolds, and that night, all were lit. A splendid harvest of grinning goblins?

They grew a much larger crop a year later. On October 29, 1994, the Keene pumpkin enthusiasts set a better world's record by lighting up more than twice that number of Halloween luminaria in the center of town. Lining the street, stacked up on three scaffolds, and ignited by about seventy volunteers, a total of 10,540 jack-o-lanterns glowed as a crowd of nearly 16,000 bystanders applauded. (What happened to the pumpkins? Tossed into trucks the next day, they were delivered to local pig farms, where—for a short time—the pigs lived high on the hog.)

Keene also has an unusual gravestone in its North Cemetery. While inscribing the epitaph for Zilpah Kilburn, who died in 1804, the engraver took advantage of an irresistible opportunity to advertise. Below her inscription he carved: "Made by Moses Wright of Rockingham price six Dollars." Yankee enterprise? Aye-uhh!

Moving eastward on Route 101, one cannot ignore Mount Monadnock. Its Indian name means "mountain that stands alone." The fact that the Indians gave it a name is in itself unusual. Indians gave names to places that were either distinctive or useful, and most mountains were neither, but Mount Monadnock, a single peak rising gently from insignificant foothills, was different. (Its Indian name was borrowed by geologists, who now universally describe similar formations as monadnocks.) From Monadnock's summit on a clear day one can view the downtown towers of Boston which are about sixty miles away. The top of Mount Monadnock is the only place in New England from which one can see parts of all six New England states.

More people climb this mountain than any other in North America, and with 200,000 persons each summer, only Mount Fujiyama in Japan has more climbers. If an auto road is ever constructed to reach the top of Mount Fujiyama, Mount Monadnock will no doubt have the most climbers in the world. Thirty miles of trails approach its summit from more than six access points but all of them require some climbing. In 1993 there were 112,536 registered climbers, a figure that reached 127,733 in 1994. Because some climbers use trails that don't require registration, these figures are minimal.

Jaffrey, New Hampshire, claims to be the home of Mount Monadnock (although in my opinion, Monadnock is the home of Jaffrey). A number of notables are buried in the well-known cemetery at Jaffrey Center, including Willa Cather, whose grave faces the view of Monadnock she loved best, and Amos Fortune, an ex-slave who was "born free in Africa, a slave in America, who purchased his liberty, professed Christianity, lived reputably, and died hopefully." He earned enough money to buy his wife's freedom and left his estate to the church and school in Jaffrey.

By way of contrast, the small Phillips Cemetery in Jaffrey's West Burying Ground goes unnoticed and is seldom visited today. That's too bad because it truly offers "rest for the weary." One of its gravestones is carved into the shape of a large (and comfortable!) armchair. That great stone chair, "fit to be the throne of a monarch of the hills," is a memorial to three generations of the Ross family who lived in this area. If spirits do sometimes return to where they earlier lived, those who departed from here can now relax in this granite chair, musing on their earlier existence while the western sun fades before them. And at this remote grave site, momentary comfort is provided to anyone else willing to accept the Ross family's kind hospitality.

New England is dappled with old burying grounds, cemeteries holding legends and lore once known to many but now to only a few. Here lie the loyalists, the patriots, the cynics and the hopeful, the children, the patriarchs, the leaders and the led. Sarah Averill's epitaph in the cemetery at Jaffrey Center reflects the New England spirit: "She done all she could."

North of Jaffrey is Peterborough. Among the silent stones in Peterborough's oldest cemetery stands that of William Diamond, who had his brief moment in the spotlight of history at the age of sixteen and who now rests quietly where few people pause. But in the early morning of April 19, 1775, while the British marched steadily toward the first head-to-head battle of the Revolutionary War, young William Diamond could not be ignored. As the world paused breathlessly with a last-minute hope that blood would not be shed, William Diamond stood ready for what might come. A mile ahead of the advancing British, Capt. John Parker turned to William, then a young drummer boy, and ordered him to summon the minutemen. Lexington Common resounded to the steady beat of William Diamond's drum, which served notice on the approaching British soldiers that "the shot heard 'round the world" was about to be fired.

Peterborough has the world's oldest free public library supported by taxation. Organized for that purpose in 1827, it was incorporated six years later when the town voted for public funds to purchase books that would be owned by the people and available without charge to all Peterborough residents. It was not that libraries were unknown before 1827. Egypt had libraries four thousand years ago. What made the Peterborough library unique was the concept that a library should belong to the people rather than to individuals, churches, corporations, guilds, or social organizations. Previously libraries were privately owned and served private interests. By creating one supported with public funds and controlled by public vote at town meetings, Peterborough invented a library that was truly both free and public.

On its 160th anniversary, the library's historical status was officially recognized by New Hampshire's governor and legislative body. By then the original collection of 499 books had grown to 43,000 plus recordings, videotapes, computers, and other educational material.

Lyman Beecher would have approved. The great evangelist exhorted his students "to pump yourselves full of your subject till you can't hold another drop, and then knock out the bung and let nature caper." Had they lived in Peterborough, they'd have gotten a head start on becoming brim full.

In his book *Six New England Villages*, photographer and author Samuel Chamberlain picked the one single town in each state that best represented an ideal New England village. The town should be small, he said, with a village green, an old church, a schoolhouse, a good inn, one general store, and a post office. It should have architectural distinction and historical significance. Its main street should be vaulted with immense trees and tapestried with wide lawns. It should be gracious, carefully tended, and hospitable.

For New Hampshire, Chamberlain selected the small town of Hancock, which lies a short distance north of Peterborough on U.S. 202. It certainly qualified. The meeting house is one of the last two in the state that are co-owned by church and town. The single inn is the oldest continuously operated inn in New Hampshire. Hancock's sixteen hundred residents are invariably gracious and hospitable.

Oddly enough, this small, idyllic town also contains an unusual astronomical structure; only seven others like it exist within the continental United States. Rising from a circular platform, great gleaming girders support an immense white disk, eighty-two feet across and cocked skyward. It's an ear that listens constantly for faint radio waves coming from outer space.

Hancock's "big ear" is part of a new compound telescope (called the Very Long Baseline Array) that is opening up fascinating frontiers in deep-space astronomy. Like others in the Array, it is controlled electronically from Array headquarters in New Mexico. The "big ear" can be rotated and tilted to listen for radio particles emitted by galaxies millions of light years from Earth. It is being used to study a mysterious region of space time "where speeding galaxies appear to stand still, huge gas clouds create an unsettling illusion that they are moving at ten times the speed of light and galactic jets twist and squirm." The Array located the largest black hole ever found in the center of an astronomical disk rotating at speeds of up to 650 miles per second in a galaxy 21 million light years away. Data accumulated by the radio telescopes will have an impact on our knowledge of space navigation, geological changes in our own world, and the movements of tectonic plates, which create earthquakes. (The antenna's presence hasn't altered Chamberlain's perception of Hancock's gentle charm. If you don't go looking for the "big ear," you won't even know it is there.)

"Highway robbery" is a quaint phrase that might be a bit out of vogue in spite of today's high cost of living. But it would have a special meaning for the workmen who built a twin-arch bridge spanning Beards Brook about 160 years ago in Hillsboro, north of Hancock on U.S. 202. Capt. Nathan Carr had it built so he could cross over from his road to one on the other side. When the bridge was done, he paid off the workmen—with funny money he had printed himself!

A picture of Captain Carr's house survives, but unfortunately there is no portrait of the man. Too bad; judging from contempo-

The Big Ear

rary accounts he was the Burt Lancaster of his time. A captain in the militia, he has been described as a tall, erect man with a military bearing and "great shoulders." He walked with the confident grace of a monarch among peasants. When he was ordered to bow his head at his sentencing, he replied defiantly, "God almighty made me to look man in the face." That got him solitary confinement for nineteen months "with his head chained down"!

No matter. Captain Carr served no man but himself—and his friends. When his crime was discovered, he refused to talk even after being sentenced to ten years in prison. Counterfeit money was found in his home and in a cave near the bridge; the printing plates were never found. No other member of his counterfeit ring was ever publicly identified.

The *History of Hillsborough, NH* admits that little was known about Captain Carr "and not much of him that is good," but with charity it concludes, "Judge him as you will; his name is here." And so is the bridge, which today remains "sound as a dollar." Maybe even more so!

The leg of Capt. Samuel Jones was born (along with the rest of him) in Hillsboro on September 30, 1777. We don't know whether or not he put his "best foot forward" at that time; nor do we know whether his later marriage to Deborah Bradford gave him a "leg up" on his career ladder. However, we do know that about the year 1800, the couple moved to Washington, New Hampshire, a small town situated northwest of Hillsboro on Route 31. According to historical markers there, it was the first incorporated town to be named after George Washington, staking its claim on action taken in the town December 13, 1776 (a small town in North Carolina may actually have an earlier claim). The town itself seethed with Tory-patriot conflicts during the Revolution. The Stone brothers, living in a red house near the common, held differing opinions. After one joined up with the British, their house was split equally down the middle. His Tory half was confiscated by the town.

While helping to move a building in 1804, Captain Jones's leg got trapped between the building and an adjacent fence, injuring it so severely that the leg had to be amputated. In a cemetery just downhill from the common, they buried Captain Jones's leg. A gravestone with the following epitaph marks the site: "Capt Samuel Jones Leg which was amputated July 7, 1804." The rest of him has eluded historians. He seems to have moved to Boston and later to New York. Reportedly his "remains" were buried in either Massachusetts or Rhode Island, but there is no certainty about his final resting place.

Back on U.S. 202 and moving northeast, Henniker proudly claims to be the only town by that name in the whole world. It is also in a

Henniker cemetery that Mary Wallace is buried. When she died, Mary Wallace was already a legend for a deed she had performed ninety-four years earlier, when she saved an entire ship, passengers, and crew from ruthless destruction by bloodthirsty pirates. She was only three days old at the time!

In the year 1720 Mary's parents were among those sailing from Londonderry, Ireland, to join earlier emigrants in Londonderry, New Hampshire. Mary was born at sea a few days before their ship reached the Massachusetts coast. Three days after her birth, disaster struck. Like a dark and roving sea panther, a pirate frigate slid up over the horizon. A shot was fired across the bow of Mary's ship. (Some say the fierce frigate flew no fateful flag, but I believe that high above her scummy scuppers the Jolly Roger grinned!)

Heaving to, the helpless emigrant vessel soon swarmed with rapacious raiders. Mustachioed and malevolent, their notorious Captain Pedro ordered the captives bound and instructed them to prepare for death. Suddenly, from below decks came the wail of infant Mary. Cutlass in hand, Captain Pedro prowled in search. Behind a closed door he found the trembling mother clutching the helpless babe. Poised to thrust, Captain Pedro hesitated—and was lost, his stony heart softened by the baby. To the fearful mother Captain Pedro made his plea: "Madam, if I am allowed to name this baby after my own mother, I promise not to harm this ship or its passengers."

Naturally, she assented. He touched the infant's tiny hand. "In the name of my sainted mother, I christen thee Ocean-Born Mary. Live long, child, and may you prosper." Returning to his own ship, Captain Pedro brought back a bolt of beautifully embroidered tapestry silk for Mary's mother. "For your daughter's bridal gown," the rogue softly growled. Then, with black sails unfurled, Captain Pedro and his cutthroats sailed off to hunt for other prey.

Mary's father, James Wilson, died shortly after the ship reached Boston. Her mother, Elizabeth, brought Mary to Londonderry, New Hampshire, where friends and fellow passengers greeted them warmly. For many years the townspeople celebrated Ocean-Born Mary's birthday as a special holiday to commemorate their deliverance from the pirates.

Ocean-Born Mary married Thomas Wallace on December 18, 1742. She wore a bridal gown made from Captain Pedro's gift. Her husband was probably dead by the time Ocean-Born Mary moved to Henniker with her four sons in 1780. Tall, with red hair, green eyes, and fair skin, she lived out her years in a lovely colonial house. Some say she built it; others claim Captain Pedro reappeared and built it for her so he could have a safe refuge from his bloody past. According to legend, he was later found under an apple tree, pierced fatally with a pirate's cutlass. The house remains. There are those who believe it to be haunted, and that Captain Pedro and his treasure are both buried there. After all, nobody has ever come up with a different explanation for the strange, coffinlike hearthstone eight feet long and three feet wide with a peculiar hole drilled down through the middle. Whatever may be under that hearthstone, we know it isn't Ocean-Born Mary. Her gravestone is in the small cemetery behind Henniker's town hall.

Southeast of Henniker along Route 114 is the small town of New Boston. In the center of the village is a triangle island around which several highways merge. A stone monument is the centerpiece, commemorating the experimental studies done in New Boston by Roger W. Babson, who arrived in New Boston around 1949. Babson and his associates "pioneered in active research for anti-gravity and a partial gravity insulator." Their Gravity Research Foundation, which he created, maintained a library about gravity. The foundation held week-long summer conferences and every year Roger Babson awarded a prize for the best essay about gravity.

Worried about the possibility of World War III, Babson chose New Boston as a safe site for him and his associates. He bought many old farms and wood lots with that in mind. After Babson's death, most of those properties were sold. The gravity library and research center were relocated to the Babson Institute in Wellesley, Massachusetts. The Babson monument was placed there by Babson himself. He also set up a trust fund to provide for continuing care of the monument and the landscape around it.

In a New Boston cemetery is a gravestone with an unusual inscription. Sevilla Jones is buried there and her epitaph reads:

"Murdered by Henry N. Sargent Jan. 13, 1854, AEt. 17 yrs. 9 mos." Below that is written:

Thus fell this lovely, blooming daughter,
By the revengeful hand—a malicious Henry,
When on her way to school he met her,
And with a six self cocked pistol shot her.

This curious epitaph in verse was probably penned by local poet Blackhawk Butterfield, who may have intended it to be the first stanza of an epic poem about the tragedy.

Sevilla Jones lived in New Boston a full century before Babson appeared on the scene. On a bright and lovely day in mid-January of 1854, when she was nearly eighteen, Sevilla walked toward her graduation ceremonies at the New Boston school. But it was a dark and ugly day for Henry Sargent. He was twenty-three and hopelessly in love with Sevilla. At first she had been pleased with his attention. He was tall, athletic, and hardy, a woodsman who could live like a "timber king." Something had changed her mind. She refused his hand and firmly rejected marriage. Henry was still on fire but Sevilla had turned into ice.

As Sevilla went toward her graduation ceremony, Henry stepped out to meet her. She said, "Good morning, Henry." He said nothing but took her by the arm. In her eyes he saw there was no longer any room for him in her heart. Henry drew one of the two pistols he carried and shot her several times in the head. She fell, lifeless. With his second pistol he shot himself. Several hours later, he too was dead.

The day was Friday the 13th.

Henry and Sevilla are buried in the same New Boston cemetery. In spite of a note found on Henry's body asking that they be buried side by side, their graves are some distance apart.

A roadside marker in Concord (east of Henniker on U.S. 202) commemorates what happened there more than two centuries ago, an event that began with the end of the Revolutionary War. Amid much travail, a federal constitution was stitched together and a critical agreement was eventually reached whereby the United States of America would finally exist, but only after nine of the thirteen colonies ratified it.

The concept of a strong central government was not easily swallowed by the colonists. Five states ratified it within three months, but Massachusetts only approved it later by the narrow vote of 187 to 168. When it was clear that New Hampshire would cast a negative vote at its convention in February of 1788, that convention was astutely adjourned until June.

By then Maryland and South Carolina had become the seventh and eighth states to accept the Constitution. Suddenly it became important to cast the decisive vote as the ninth state to ratify the Constitution. After four days of torrid debate, New Hampshire won its place in history with a close affirmative vote of fifty-seven to forty-six. The secretary of the convention recorded the time as precisely 1:00 P.M. (just in case Virginia later tried to edge into that honorable slot. However, Patrick Henry's stubborn objections delayed Virginia's acceptance until it was too late). The date was June 21, 1788, the day the United States of America was born at last!

The State House in Concord is America's oldest state capitol building in which the legislative body continues to meet in its original chambers. It houses the largest state legislative body in America (and the third largest among all English-speaking legislative bodies in the world). Even among those who live and work in Concord, few are aware of the unusual career of John Parker Hale, one the four men whose statues decorate the State House lawn. In 1775 John Adams's "Rules for the Regulation of the Navy" (drawn up in the Continental Congress) permitted up to twelve lashes for any sailor who was drunk or used foul language. Those who have more recently worn "bell-bottom trousers and coats of Navy blue" might like to know that back in 1850 it was John Parker Hale who managed to outlaw the use of flogging as a punishment for sailors in our navy.

Hale was also outspoken in Congress against slavery. He was publicly so opposed to slavery that in 1846 he was elected to the U.S. Senate on that very issue, probably the nation's first antislavery senator. Hale waged such a campaign against slavery that Vice

President John Calhoun once said he "would sooner argue with a maniac from Bedlam than with the Senator from New Hampshire on the question of slavery."

Later in his career John Parker Hale was appointed ambassador to Spain by President Lincoln. One morning shortly before he was to depart for Spain with his family, Hale met with the president to discuss his future duties as ambassador. On a personal note Hale revealed to the president that he had a private reason for wanting to take his family abroad: Hale's daughter Lucy had become secretly engaged to a young man whom Hale disliked and he hoped the separation would bring Lucy to her senses. Hale's dislike for the young man was well-founded. On that very evening Lucy's suitor assassinated President Abraham Lincoln.

The first time that a fire was quenched by man-made rain occurred in Concord, which may not initially seem to be a likely site for experiments in rain making. On October 29, 1947, the General Electric Company in Schenectady flew planes over a forest fire burning in Concord. Dry ice from the planes seeded cumulus clouds. The resulting rain helped extinguish the fire, but since a natural rain followed soon after the experiment, the effectiveness of the seeding remained in doubt.

On a wide and quiet street not far from the State House there is a charming residence that easily evokes a nostalgic past. It's a neighborly structure with a veranda where Mickey Rooney might still share a porch glider and a pitcher of lemonade with Judy Garland (just before he shouts, "Why don't we put on a show?") The Reverend Timothy Walker House is the oldest in Concord and believed to be the first house built north of Massachusetts (although because of conflicting land grants, no one really knew where that border was located). A stockade was erected around the house in 1746, turning it into a garrison house. Behind the stockade walls, Walker's family and those of eight neighbors mounted their defense against the invasions of French and Indian war parties. In a garrison house, everyone crowded together for mutual protection whenever Indian raids were expected, usually during the warm summer months. Families living in a cramped garrison house during the summer heat had few comforts (and no indoor plumbing). Small wonder they looked forward to winter and their own homes! With its renewed possibility of a late Indian raid, how they must have detested and dreaded the last warm spell of weather that so delights us now—Indian summer! With its revival of Indian terror and a return to garrison life, they sang no songs of praise to Indian summer.

Some of Reverend Walker's stockade was still standing in 1772 when nineteen-year-old Benjamin Thompson arrived. Sponsored by the good reverend to teach school in Concord, young Thompson met, courted, and (within three months) married the reverend's daughter Sarah, a rich widow in her thirties. Through the Walkers, young Thompson met and was favored by the royal governors of Massachusetts and New Hampshire. With the hoofbeats of rebellion sounding along country lanes, it became unpopular to be known as a good friend of the Crown's rulers. Benjamin Thompson was accused of being a rebel to the state. Though not proven, the accusation was enough to make him depart from Concord in haste.

Under scrutiny again in Massachusetts, he sailed for England. He was knighted by King George III and later made a count of the Holy Roman Empire. Allowed to choose his own titular name, he thumbed his nose at Concord by electing to call himself Count Rumford, Rumford being an earlier name for Concord.

His name may not be familiar, but you owe something to him if you now own or plan to build a fireplace. This adventurer, opportunist, and ladies' man is best known to the world today as a scientist. Studying the flow of heated air currents, he designed the first open fireplace that did not spill smoke out into the room. His design elements of smoke shelf, throat, and damper are still in use. He worked out the proper balance between the opening of a fireplace and the size of its chimney throat. He utilized heat radiation by slanting the back and beveling the sides of the firebox. His research continues to affect more lives than we realize.

One final word about the count. Despite his protests to those who drummed him out of New Hampshire, Benjamin Thompson had in fact been a spy for the British. As such he can be credited with another first. On May 6, 1775, Thompson wrote a letter to British general Thomas Gage inside Boston. Written in black ink, its contents seemed harmless enough to the sentries outside of

Boston who read it and allowed it to pass into the city, where it reached General Gage. By prearrangement with Thompson, Gage used a ferrous sulfate solution to bring out the secret-ink message Thompson had included in the letter. Thompson had outlined in detail all of the American military plans. His was the first secret-ink message known by historians to have been sent during the Revolutionary War.

A few miles southeast of Concord, in what has been described as an abandoned graveyard in North Pembroke, lies the grave of Harmon Fife, who invented the revolver in 1835. This news may come as a surprise to those who thought the revolver was the brainchild of Samuel Colt. Some area residents are still convinced that after Fife invented the revolver, Samuel Colt stole Fife's plans. The epitaph on Fife's gravestone (in which his first name is misspelled as Hermon) contains the following verse:

> Here lies the man, never beat by a plan.
> Straight was his aim and sure of his game.
> Never was a lover but invented the revolver.

Harmon Fife's invention was handmade by him in 1835. Approximately ten inches long, the revolver was cocked by squeezing back on the trigger guard and then fired by using the trigger itself. His original seven-shot cylinder had to be rotated by hand. Samuel Colt had applied for a patent prior to 1836 for a revolver of a much more advanced design in which the cylinder was rotated by simply cocking the hammer.

As for the line in Fife's epitaph that he "never was a lover," there seems to be no existing information about it one way or the other.

Still farther southeast of Concord is Exeter, founded in 1638. Early leaders had been banished from Massachusetts for heresy. During the Revolution, Exeter became New Hampshire's capital (there were simply too many Tories in Portsmouth), and in 1776 the Provincial Congress in Exeter adopted the first state constitution, creating by that act the first independent state government in all of the thirteen colonies.

One of the odd moments in Exeter's history centers on a long, old-fashioned house that still exists at the intersection of Front and Winter streets. Built around 1740, it first served as a tavern or inn and later became a hat factory. In the last years of that century, it became the headquarters of the "White Cap Society." The founder of the society was Rainsford Rogers who appeared in Exeter sometime around 1798. Rogers claimed he had the power to possess and control both good and evil spirits at his pleasure. (He had made similar claims earlier in New Jersey, but news traveled slowly in those days.) Rogers managed to convince a number of astute financiers in Exeter that with the help of his special powers, he and his spirits could locate for them a "large subterranean treasure of great value." Lured on by his glib tongue, they slipped secretly through the dark nights, following him to various locations where they dug, and dug, and dug—always in vain. During those nocturnal expeditions, it was essential that they all wear white caps.

Rogers eventually convinced the White Cap Society that their failure to find the elusive treasure could be overcome only by buying a special (and very expensive) divining rod which had to be purchased in Philadelphia. Dazzled by cupidity, the White Cap Society raised the required amount and turned it over to Rogers. He promptly borrowed a saddle and bridle from one of his dupes, mounted, rode off—and was never heard from again.

A short distance toward the coast from Exeter is Hampton Falls. The First Baptist Church, right on the town common, has a tall, slender spire that's hard to miss. At the very top is an ambiguous ornament. To some people it is a very large champagne bottle, placed there by builders (who normally followed a tradition of tying a small tree to the uppermost ridge of any building they worked on). Still another theory is that when money was needed to finish the steeple in the 1850s, a brewery in Portsmouth offered it if the symbol of their product was placed at the top. Is the five-and-a-half-foot-high ornament really a giant beer bottle? At least one pastor is reported to have subscribed to that belief, even though the brewer in Portsmouth was still a vendor when the ornament was emplaced. Church officials today smile at the legends. Topping the spire is an ordinary finial, an architectural form often used to soften the blunt ending of a rod, a pole, or—as in this case—a slender pinnacle. It was popular long before anyone invented beer bottles, and whoever did that may have simply copied the shape of a finial.

New Hampshire is also called "the granite state," and with good reason. Large chunks of it are heaped up all over the place. So why should another pile of boulders attract any attention? In Salem—between Exeter and the Massachusetts border—a bunch of granite rocks has done just that.

America's Stonehenge, located in Salem, was originally called Mystery Hill. It may be more of a mystery than an archaeological find; no one is absolutely certain about what it is. It has chambers, stone walls, a "sacrificial table" with a carved drainage channel around the outer edge, a sump pit, water channels, and standing stones, all of which appear to be the remnants of an ancient civilization. Some experts believe the site was built by Irish Culdee monks fleeing from savage Vikings in the eleventh century. Unfortunately, the removal of tons of stone from the site in the 1860s to build dams and sewers in nearby towns may have destroyed valuable archaeological evidence.

One of the alternate theories about the site revolves around Jonathan Pettee, who acquired the land in 1823. Although not much is known about Pettee, he was believed by many to be an eccentric who created the stone structures himself. He was rumored to have used the stone huts to store barrels of cider, or to hide runaway slaves moving along the Underground Railroad, or perhaps as a place where he could hide from the law.

Pettee did build a house on his land and may well have added to the stone structures there. But the intricate arrangement of the slabs and boulders imply techniques not used by nineteenth-century builders. Carbon dating shows that charcoal at the site is at least four thousand years old. An elaborate drainage system had been chiseled into the ledge and the huge stones surrounding the area appear to be aligned with solar and lunar movements. These factors tend to support the most interesting theory about America's Stonehenge—that an ancient people, unrecorded in history, once lived there, charting the seasons and worshiping their unknown gods. After more than a half century of exploration, analysis, and debate, however, the site remains a puzzle.

Backtracking to Concord and heading north, there's a larger-than-life memorial in Boscawen to Hannah Dustin, who engineered the deaths of ten sleeping Indians at that spot. Sculptured in off-the-shoulder dishabille, a tomahawk in her one hand is matched by scalps dangling from the other. (Periodically both get painted red by unknown persons who may simply be interested in historical accuracy.)

What led to that murderous event started on March 15, 1697, in Haverhill, Massachusetts, during an Indian raid. Hannah's husband, working in the field with seven of their children, chose to herd them to safety at a garrison house, though it meant abandoning his wife and infant child in their cabin. Twenty-seven settlers, including Hannah's baby, lay dead among the ruins of the raid. Hannah and her midwife, Mary Neff, were among eleven captives forced into a cruel march north. Fearful of pursuit, the large raiding party split up.

Hannah and Mary became captives of an Indian family consisting of five adults, seven children, and a third prisoner, young Samuel Leonardson. By March 30 they had reached an island around which the Contoocook River swirled into the Merrimack River. Here Hannah Dustin made her move toward freedom. Somehow she stole a hatchet. Late that night while their captors slept, Hannah killed two of the warriors with her tomahawk. Armed now with two more hatchets, the three captives killed eight more Indians. Only a wounded Indian woman and a young boy escaped into the woods.

Hardly had the three started down river by canoe when Hannah insisted they return to the island. Massachusetts was paying bounties for Indian scalps and they had forgotten to scalp those they had slain. The scalp of an Indian child under ten was worth only one-fifth of the money offered for an adult scalp; still, the scalps of four adults and six children would bring a tidy sum which a prudent colonial housewife could not ignore. Back again in their canoe, they fled down the Merrimack toward Haverhill, sighting at last the familiar terrain around the ruins of that town.

Word of their exploit spread. The Massachusetts General Court, which was in session, voted to award the Dustins twenty-five pounds. Naturally they paid the money to Hannah's husband.

If you are browsing around in Webster, New Hampshire (a short distance west of Boscawen), and happen to see a Swiss chalet– type house on top of a hill, it might be the one that used to be a covered bridge. Originally the covered bridge spanned the Blackwater River at Sweatts Mills, but it was condemned in 1909 and given to the owner of some land on the north side of the river. When the bridge was torn down, timbers and boards were moved across the river to a new location and used to build a quaint replica of a Swiss chalet. It is now a permanent year-round residence. (Not much goes to waste in New Hampshire.)

Up the road a piece along U.S. 3 is Franklin, which publicly claims that the eminent Daniel Webster was born there. As a matter of fact, Daniel Webster was born in Salisbury long before Franklin had come into existence. When the town of Franklin was established in 1828, it incorporated the part of Salisbury where Webster had been born, thus depriving Salisbury of its major claim to fame (which many local residents continue to point out).

A nationally recognized statesman, lawyer, and orator, Daniel Webster is probably New Hampshire's favorite son. Around him swirl many stories and legends, mostly about his ability to sway listeners with his words. According to legend, he could wring real tears from weeping willow trees. His eloquence made him the foremost speaker in the U.S. Senate, which was then renowned for its oratory.

In his poetic legend *The Devil and Daniel Webster*, Stephen Vincent Benét told of the border country, where Massachusetts joins Vermont and New Hampshire. That's where a dirt-poor New Hampshire farmer named Jabez Stone made a pact with the devil by trading his soul for seven years of wealth. But when the seven years ended, Jabez demanded a trial by judge and jury to determine whether such a contract was legal. The devil assented, provided he got to pick the judge and jury. And Daniel Webster agreed to represent Jabez Stone.

To preside over the hearing, the devil picked a hanging judge from the Salem witch trials—the only judge who never repented his decisions. His jury consisted of American villains, pirates, stranglers, renegades who tortured early settlers, and government officials who had broken men on the wheel. The devil had indeed stacked the deck!

But Daniel Webster recognized the one thing that all of them had in common. All were men with the memory of what it meant to be men. He spoke eloquently to that memory. The devil lost! His hand-picked jury of villains ruled in favor of Jabez Stone.

So Jabez Stone kept his soul but the devil got his revenge. Knowing of Webster's great desire to become president, the devil swore it would never happen. He kept his vow. Still, that didn't bother the people of New Hampshire. They thought then as they do today: it's a fine thing to be elected president of the United States but it's an even greater honor to be born in New Hampshire.

The central street in Belmont looks very much like any Main Street in any small New England town where small changes are common. There is a dairy bar now where the post office existed in 1960. And it was in that post office that Richard P. Pavlik made his mistake.

In November 1960 John F. Kennedy was elected president of the United States, scheduled to take office the following January. On December 11 he was at his father's mansion in Palm Beach, Florida. His wife and two children were there with him. The Palm Beach weather was perfect. Two Secret Service agents stood at the driveway entrance as guards for the president-elect. A motorcycle policeman lounged nearby to keep pedestrians moving if that became necessary.

Shortly before ten o'clock, a car slowed down and parked across from the Kennedy mansion. (Nothing illegal or suspicious about doing that in December of 1960.) The driver of the car was Richard P. Pavlik, who had driven down from his home in Belmont, New Hampshire. Determined to assassinate John F. Kennedy, Pavlik had rigged seven sticks of dynamite in his car. They could be exploded by pressing a simple switch. Pavlik knew that the president-elect would be attending Mass that morning. The Kennedy car was already parked on the roadway a short distance in front of Pavlik.

Once Kennedy entered his car, Pavlik intended to smash into the Kennedy car and explode the dynamite. According to a later Secret Service report, there was enough dynamite to blow up a small mountain, and unquestionably it would have wiped out Senator Kennedy, his family, Pavlik, and all of the Secret Service agents, as well as anybody else nearby.

The explosion never occurred. Kennedy came out onto the veranda. As Pavlik watched, Kennedy was joined by his wife, his daughter, and several nieces and nephews. Appalled by their presence, Pavlik sat frozen. As he later stated, "I did not wish to harm her or the children. I decided to get him at church or some place later."

It was already too late. Secret Service agents had been hard at work trying to locate Richard Pavlik. Three days later they tracked him to Palm Beach. Within twenty-four hours, Pavlik was under arrest. In his possession at the time were photographs of the Kennedy mansion, the church Kennedy attended, and the layout of streets around it. On at least one occasion Pavlik had been in the church while Kennedy was there.

Where had he made his mistake? In the post office at Belmont, Pavlik was overheard making threats against John F. Kennedy. A postal inspector reported those threats to the Secret Service in Washington. That agency began tracking Pavlik and, fortunately, caught up to him before he could make a second attempt to kill John F. Kennedy.

Kennedy had two years and eleven more months to live before another, less compassionate assassin ended his life in Dallas, Texas.

In Belmont you are close to New Hampshire's lakes region. Wolfeboro is on the eastern edge of New Hampshire's largest lake, Lake Winnipesaukee. Here is where colonial governor John Wentworth built the first summer home in America—the first, that is, if we decide to ignore the migratory movements of New England Indians who went from winter quarters to summer camps. But we should give Governor Wentworth credit for starting a trend that is still in fashion. Based on his summer residence (which no longer exists) Lake Winnipesaukee can justifiably claim to be America's first summer resort.

Driving up the western fringe of the lakes region, pause for just a moment on the road that connects Ashland with West Center Harbor. Three miles east of Ashland is the exact geographic center of New Hampshire. If a map of New Hampshire were made out of stiff cardboard, this is where it would balance on a pencil point. Don't bother looking for a roadside marker, though.

Another sign of stability exists up the road a piece at North Woodstock. On the west side of Route 3 (by Wayne's Market) is the Rock of Ages Church. Its congregation would have to be the smallest in America. The building consists of one tiny room reached by some rickety steps. It is perched on top of a large boulder and that boulder sits on top of a hill. The Rock of Ages Church may be the most precariously balanced religious edifice in the nation. Inside is a small altar, a bookstand with an open Bible, and numerous photographs or religious artifacts grouped around the walls. The small room is just large enough to hold a preacher, a bride, and groom, along with their maid of honor, best man, and a few witnesses (provided none of them are seated). One couple married there because the bride's parents had been wedded in the same church many years earlier.

The landscape gave birth to the church. Sometime in the early 1940s, a visitor told the landowner that the hillside reminded him of the Holy Land. The owner and his daughter then constructed some paths depicting various stages in the life of Christ. One day the owner saw a nun kneeling before a creche in the pouring rain. He decided to build a suitable shelter, which evolved into the Rock of Ages Church. Nondenominational, the church is open to the public (and donations are accepted).

On the way up to Mount Washington along Route 16 is a small community that decided in 1800 to call itself Adams in honor of the election of John Adams. Twenty-eight years later John Quincy Adams lost the presidential election to Andrew Jackson, and the town of Adams promptly changed its name to Jackson. That's been its name ever since. (I guess presidential elections don't mean as much nowadays as they once did.)

Moving westward to the Connecticut River and then downstream, you will see a constant flow of traffic passing over a cov-

The Rock of Ages Church

ered bridge. The Cornish-Windsor Bridge was built in 1866 and has recently been renovated. Originally a private toll bridge, it was purchased by New Hampshire in 1936 and tolls were collected until 1943. (The sign on the bridge still says, WALK YOUR HORSE OR PAY A TWO DOLLAR FINE.) The bridge is 460 feet long. Using two spans to cross the river, it is the longest two-span covered bridge in the world and has been described as having an "unusual timber lattice truss construction." For the cautious driver/photographer, watch where you park.

How are costs shared between Vermont and New Hampshire

when bridges across the Connecticut River need repair? Vermont pays for that portion of the bridge that overhangs Vermont. The Cornish-Windsor Bridge was repaired in 1989, and Vermont paid only 5 percent of the cost. The only remaining toll bridge over the river connects Charlestown, New Hampshire, with Springfield, Vermont. A private toll bridge when New Hampshire bought it, New Hampshire owns the entire bridge, retains all of the tolls, and maintains the whole structure.

South of Claremont and on the east side of Route 12, a restaurant named Indian Shutters serves excellent food at modest prices—but the real oddity lies in the building itself. Built in the 1790s (when it was known as the Colonel Parker Inn), it was a stopping place for travelers along the John Stark Highway, which explains why the building has its back facing Route 12. Its current name comes from the still-extant wood panels that were slid across the windows by early occupants during Indian raids. Not much protection from arrows, but the shutters made it impossible for the raiders to see their targets.

The cellar is believed to be the deepest residential one in New Hampshire. The ceiling down there is ten feet from the floor, about as high up as a basketball hoop. In the part of the cellar that is now a lounge area, massive wooden beams stretch horizontally from sidewall to sidewall across the ceiling. Their strength was needed during the period when stagecoaches, weighing over a ton apiece, were housed in the space above.

Charlestown is downriver from Claremont. Originally it was simply Fort Number Four, an armed outpost to protect colonists. In 1747 its thirty-man garrison was attacked by four hundred French and Indians. The French commander thought the overwhelming odds would result in a massacre of the defenders and offered to accept a peaceful surrender. Capt. Phineas Stevens replied that his men were not afraid to die and the battle was on. It raged for three days before the attackers abandoned their effort and withdrew. Hearing of the valiant defense, a British naval officer in Boston, Sir Charles Knowles, presented Captain Stevens with an elegant sword. In return, Fort Number Four eventually named itself Charlestown.

Off a short distance to the southeast are the small towns of Acworth and Langdon. Acworth has a cemetery that is known largely because of what happened to the corpse of Bezaleel Beckwith, who died at the age of forty-three and was buried there on October 31, 1824. Thirteen days later, his body was stolen from the grave. The disappearance of Beckwith's body probably had nothing to do with the fact that his burial had taken place on Halloween or that grave-robbers waited thirteen nights before digging up his corpse. This theft took place back when medical schools were beginning to flourish and cadavers for dissection and anatomical studies were in short supply.

The monument marking Beckwith's grave site was destroyed by "person or persons unknown" in April of 1853. The current monument contains this inscription:

> *This stone tells the death of Bezaleel Beckwith, not where his body lies. He died Oct. 31, 1824, AE 43. The 13th night after his body was stolen from the grave. Erected by the friends of the deceased in Acworth in place of one destroyed by some ruthless hand in April, 1853.*

The Prentiss Bridge in Langdon is on a short lane right next to the Cheshire Turnpike Road. An earlier bridge had been built in the fall of 1791 but was replaced by the current bridge in 1874. Only thirty feet long, the Prentiss Bridge is the shortest covered bridge still standing on public property and is listed on the Register of Historical Landmarks. It was active until 1954, when the new roadway was built next to it. Somewhat dilapidated now, it still provided a colorful setting for a wedding in 1985.

New Hampshire is a narrow state with the Connecticut River on its western border. Inevitably, bridges played a large role in local legends. Many a bridge disappeared while its history remained alive. Though it no longer exists (look for the historical marker on Route 12), the first bridge spanning the Connecticut River at any point bordering New Hampshire was built across the great falls between North Walpole, New Hampshire, and Bellows Falls, Vermont in 1784–85. Under a special act of the New Hampshire legislature, Enoch Hale of Rindge was granted the exclusive right to construct and maintain a toll bridge allowing direct passage from Boston to Canada. No other bridge could be built within two miles above or below his. Tolls were exacted for men, animals, and stagecoaches: each passenger on foot, three cents; each horse and rider, six cents; wagon drawn by one horse with driver, ten cents; mail stage with passengers included, twenty-five cents; horses four cents each; sheep, hogs, calves, and goats, ten cents the score or a half cent each. Obviously Hale's bridge was a moneymaker!

Like many wealthy men, Enoch Hale had occasional cash flow problems. He mortgaged the bridge to a wealthy Englishman, Frederick W. Geyer, who spent his summers in a mansion up on the steep hill at the east end of the bridge. The conditions were that if any payment day ended without payment being received, ownership of the bridge would immediately pass from Hale to Geyer. Geyer really wanted that bridge and hoped that someday payment

The bridge that love lost

would fail to arrive in time at his Boston office. One autumn day he got his wish. A day too late, Hale's son arrived with payment in hand. Geyer would accept neither the money nor the excuses. The bridge now belonged to him.

Young Hale had left by stage in plenty of time to make the payment in Boston the next day. At the inn where he was to spend the night, he suddenly discovered that sitting across the room was the wife from whom he had separated some years before. As they talked together, the differences that had earlier parted them slowly disappeared, forgotten in their blissful reunion. Forgotten too was the need for him to catch the first stage to Boston the next morning.

Love conquers all—but not always!

MAINE

Like all New England states except Vermont, Maine can be accessed by sea as well as by land. Sailing ships traveling toward England used the prevailing winds blowing eastward and the downstream flow of the Gulf Stream current to speed them along. (The effect of the Gulf Stream was first noticed by Benjamin Franklin, who wondered why ships sailing to England made a faster trip than did those returning along the same route.) Travelers heading east into Maine are still going "down east." There seems to be no comparable term for westbound travelers, although those heading for Boston from Portland are said to be going "up to Boston."

Any curious traveler looking for the unusual might be advised to enter Maine from New Hampshire's Kancamagus Highway and then head northeast toward the junction of Routes 5 and 35 in Lynchville. There, New England's most renowned signpost provides specific mileage on arrows pointing toward Norway (14 miles), Paris (15 miles), Denmark (23 miles), Naples (23 miles), Sweden (25 miles), Poland (27 miles), Mexico (37 miles), Peru (46 miles), and China (94 miles). All are towns in Maine. You *can* get there from here!

The three towns with Scandinavian names were not so named simply because their pioneers were Scandinavian. When the town of Denmark was incorporated in 1807, Americans favored the Danish seamen who had just fought bravely against a superior British navy. Sweden became a town in 1813, when the European Sweden was a Napolean dependency struggling for its freedom. Steep waterfalls exist at the end of the village of Norway, and the Indian word for "falls" is "norridge." The petition for incorporation asked that the town be named "Norage," and that got twisted into "Norway" through the crude spelling of pioneer times.

Just a few miles north of Norway lies Paris. Paris Hill is certainly worth a visit. Many who have been there believe Paris Hill to be the most beautiful small town in New England. Once an important stage stop on the route between Portland and Montreal, Paris Hill is off the beaten path of travelers today. Paris Hill's oddity, the Old Stone Jail, was built in 1822 as a county jail from granite blocks quarried in the town of Oxford and dragged by oxen over the snow to Paris Hill. Though the blocks look pretty massive, four prisoners managed to pry one loose on the north wall around 1834. Three escaped and were never recaptured. The fourth (perhaps overfed) became stuck in the wall. Unable to advance or retreat, he was discovered the next morning still wedged in the opening. Today the small stone structure serves as the Hamlin Memorial Hall. Its lower floor houses a library while the upper one is a museum displaying American primitive art, local minerals, Hamlin memorabilia, and a sign originally posted outside the jail asking passersby not to speak to the prisoners. Above the current ground-floor entrance is the original second-floor doorway. Bars are still in place across the windows.

Visitors to Paris Hill are advised take a two-stop side trip northward. In Bryant Pond, a sign on a small building reads: BRYANT POND TELEPHONE COMPANY. It is possible to stand on the porch and look through the windows at the switchboard and other equipment of what was once the smallest privately owned telephone company in the United States—and the last to use hand-cranked magnetos instead of a dial system. Phone calls were a nickel. For twenty-five years the phones were attended, day and night, within the living room of that house. Still visible is the sofa used by the person working the night shift. Ceremonial dinners at Thanksgiving and Christmas were served at a large table in the living room so that callers could be answered promptly. Retired from active duty in 1983, the phone building was converted into a museum three years later. The original telephone pole still stands outside, topped with archaic glass insulators.

Farther north at Byron, gold is still being panned out of the Swift River. Equipment can be rented locally and lessons on how to do it are available for beginners. Most of the color found today is "flour gold," or small pieces ground off larger nuggets. However, larger nuggets can still be found. Mining goes as far back as the eighteenth century. Later records have miners working there in the 1830s, and strikes then were very real. People infected with gold fever neglected their farms. Some local miners who went to the 1849 gold rush in California returned because they thought they could do better in Byron. Byron is said to be the site of the country's very first gold strike. Imagine that—the country's oldest, and still not all panned out.

Somewhat east of Byron is the town of Wilton. In the residential area on High Street is a small building that houses a rather unusual canning factory owned by four generations of the Wells family. It is said to be the world's only cannery for dandelion greens, and the only fiddlehead fern cannery in the United States. In the early days, dandelions were trucked from Rangeley, where they were "dug in the wild," washed, blanched, and sealed in brine. Today some of the greens are harvested about four times a year on the Wells' own farm. Others are shipped in from brokers around New England. The Wells' fiddleheads are marketed in various specialty shops (although Shop and Save in Maine also carries them). Orders come from all over the United States, mostly from people who have lived in Maine for whom nothing can compare to a mess of dandelion greens cooked up with boiled potatoes and salt pork. (If that's not to your taste, try dandelion spoon bread, creamed dandelions, a dandelion casserole, or a dandelion omelet. Recipes are available from the Wells family, who also advise customers that "the water dandelions are cooked in is full of vitamins. It should not be thrown away, but saved to put in soups or drink." How about a dandelion Bloody Mary?)

The nearby Wilton Home and Farm Museum was once known as the Bass Boarding House, built by the famous shoemaker to house employees. Among the exhibits is a life-size figure of Sylvia Hardy, "The Maine Giantess," born in Wilton in 1823. Sylvia Hardy was just shy of eight feet tall and weighed four hundred pounds when she was forty years old. She could cradle a baby in one hand. She was eventually persuaded to join P. T. Barnum's museum in New York, where she was billed as the "Tallest Lady in the World." The Wilton Museum displays a gown she wore at that time. (According to some sources, Barnum ordered her to wear built-up shoes and to have wide vertical stripes sewn into her gowns to emphasize her height.) She died in 1888 and is buried in the Wilton Lakeview Cemetery. Her coffin was placed on a dolly and wheeled to the grave site.

Henry Bass, a Wilton cobbler who made sturdy shoes for sturdy New England farmers, popularized the shoe style now known worldwide as a loafer. (The museum displays a letter from a customer who was returning a pair of Bass shoes because he "could not seem to wear them out.") Bass made specialty items also, such as the insulated hiking boots used on both of Admiral Byrd's expeditions to the South Pole and the lightweight flying boots Charles Lindbergh wore on his historic flight. In 1936 Bass was shown a Norwegian slipper moccasin and secured permission to redesign it for the American market. The Bass Weejun got its name from the last two syllables of "Norwegian" and soon became the most popular hand-sewn moccasin ever made.

Moving eastward toward Skowhegan, any connoisseur of curiosities should visit Madison, a town first inhabited by Norridgewock Indians. The French once used Madison as an outpost to block further British colonial expansion up the Kennebec River toward Canada. The Indians led by Father Rasles, a Jesuit missionary who lived with them, constantly raided British settlements downriver. On August 23, 1724, a strong British force retaliated, taking the village by surprise, killing Father Rasles and slaughtering most of the natives. A few survivors melted away and practiced staying out of sight along the upper Kennebec. Today a plaque on a boulder and a lone memorial to the French priest who led the Indians are the only reminders of the incident.

Fifty-one years later in 1774, Gen. Benedict Arnold gathered an army of men together at Fort Western (now the city of Augusta) to head up the Kennebec River, cross into Canada, and attack the British stronghold at Quebec. One of those soldiers was young Aaron Burr. Legend says that a lovely Indian princess, Jacataqua, caught sight of him at Fort Western, fell in love with him, and traveled with him to Quebec, where he abandoned her and her unborn child. During the struggle to reach Quebec, food for the starving men is said to have mysteriously appeared. A canoe appeared just in time for some floundering soldiers to save themselves. A map left in a cleft stick pointed the correct path to the disoriented men. As Arnold's tattered and starving band approached their goal, a group of Indians suddenly appeared and offered to join them. Apparently they had been his unseen allies from the start. Knowing of Arnold's mistrust of Indians, they had decided to have Jacataqua travel openly with his army while they used her information about conditions to provide invisible assistance whenever they could. Jacataqua needed an acceptable excuse to tag along, so she conveniently "fell in love" with handsome Aaron Burr. Without the help of the Indians, Arnold's men might never have reached Quebec. The attack on Quebec failed, but it was not the failure of the Indians. Why would this small band of Indians have devoted themselves to helping Arnold's army? One theory is that they were Norridgewock Indians who hated the British for their 1724 massacre. Whatever they could do to help the Americans against the British would be their revenge. If that's true, Jacataqua deserves a better legend than the one she got.

Speaking of unusual Indians, the world's largest wooden Indian is in Skowhegan. Sculpted by Bernard "Blackie" Langlais in 1969, the Skowhegan Indian is sixty-two feet tall and stands on a base twenty feet high. Dressed in buckskin, he holds a fish spear in one hand and a wooden weir in the other. The sculpture is dedicated to the Maine Indians, "the first people to use these lands in peaceful ways."

The movie *On Golden Pond* garnered several Academy Awards, and the lake in New Hampshire where it was filmed proudly claims itself to be Golden Pond. But the author, Ernest Thompson (who won an Oscar for his screenplay), spent his summers in an idyllic setting on Great Pond, south of Skowhegan and the largest of the Belgrade Lakes. He wrote his bittersweet story of an aging couple at their lakeside cottage in Maine with Great Pond in mind. His character Charlie is based on a real-life mailman who delivered mail by boat from dock to dock. If you've seen the movie, you can now view the setting that inspired it.

East of the Belgrade Lakes, the "Two Cent" Swinging Bridge still swings in Waterville. It hangs over the Kennebec River, a walkway connecting Waterville with the town across the river, Winslow. The bridge was originally built for people who lived in Waterville but walked across the bridge to reach the Scott Paper Company plant on the other side. Built in 1903 to replace a wooden bridge that had washed away, the seven hundred–foot steel suspension span is anchored on both banks with heavy cables to reduce side-to-side swaying. Until 1962, each person using the bridge was charged two cents to cross. The Ticonic Foot Bridge (its official name), the nation's only known toll footbridge, has been closed to traffic since 1973.

Fort Halifax, on the Winslow side of the river, consists of a single square two-story building built from heavy timbers with the second floor jutting out over the first one so defenders inside could fire down on attackers below. The Fort Halifax blockhouse is the oldest blockhouse in the nation. It took thirteen men eighty-two days to build the fort in 1754, using hand-hewn timbers fastened with wooden dowels. Their wages were "provisions and drink." Erected as a defense during the French and Indian Wars, Fort Halifax was never attacked, either by the French or by any Indians. After the Treaty of Paris in 1763, the fort was abandoned and dismantled— except for the single blockhouse.

Oddly enough, this oldest blockhouse in the nation is also the newest! On April 1 and 2, 1984, flood waters on the Kennebec inundated the point of land where the blockhouse stood. When the water reached its second story, the blockhouse simply floated.

Fort Halifax Blockhouse

Swept downstream, it struck a railroad bridge in Augusta and broke up. Parts were carried still farther downriver. Massive hand-hewn timbers washed ashore all the way from Augusta to the ocean. Ultimately forty of them were recovered, as was the door, most of the second-story floor, and the historic bronze plaque.

Every recovered timber was studied before reconstruction of the blockhouse began. Over the years some earlier repairs had been made, but now only the twenty-two beams dating from the original structure were retained. New beams to replace missing timbers were hand-hewn from the same wood species originally used and were cut to the original dimensions. To prevent possible future loss, the blockhouse was pinned to its site by hidden concrete-filled steel pipes set twenty feet into the ground. With this restoration, the existing Fort Halifax blockhouse became both the oldest and the newest blockhouse in the United States.

The old Fort Hill Cemetery is also in Winslow, not far from the blockhouse. Many of the gravestones have deteriorated so badly that the epitaphs can no longer be read. Buried under one is Ebenezer Wood, who died November 2, 1837. The inscription (no longer legible but still remembered by those who copied it earlier) named him as "Beza Wood." His epitaph, carved onto an old stone somewhere in the Fort Hill Cemetery, would not have pleased him:

> Here lies one Wood, encased in wood,
> One Wood within another.
> The outer wood is very good,
> We cannot praise the other.

Moving eastward from Winslow, plan a stop at Bangor, which contains a number of unusual attractions, including a Civil War memorial built in 1963. Located near the entrance to the Mount Hope Cemetery, the striking bronze sculpture (with an unusual modern design) is dedicated to the Second Maine Regiment of Volunteers. A completely different style of sculpture portrays Paul Bunyon, the legendary lumberjack, gazing across Main Street toward the Penobscot River. He stands thirty-one feet tall, weighs thirty-seven hundred pounds, and is made of fiberglass braced internally with steel. (Did you know that his wife's name was Minnie? Or that this mythical lumberjack was allegedly born there in 1834?)

Bangor got its name by accident. Reverend Seth Noble was commissioned to present an application for the new town, requesting that it be named Sunbury. Noble's favorite hymn was called "Bangor" and he exasperated his congregation by scheduling it often during church services. Unfortunately, he happened to be humming it at the time he presented the town's petition. When the recording clerk asked for the name of the new town, Noble thought he was being asked for the name of the tune he was humming. Sunbury became Bangor and its residents have learned to live with it.

However, few people in Bangor can explain another name that appears quite often in the area: Norumbega. The oddity surrounding the name began in 1568 when Sir John Hawkins marooned

David Ingram and two other English sailors at Tampico on the Gulf of Mexico. They made their way north as far as Maine, perhaps the first white men to tread on Maine soil. A French trading vessel later picked them up and returned them to Europe. Ingram wrote a colorful tale of his adventures, in which he described the fabulous Indian village of Norumbega, locating it near where Bangor now stands. (The name can be interpreted as Penobscot Indian for "still-water-between-falls.") Ingram described Indian monarchs being carried through the streets while seated on golden chairs. He saw furs, precious stones, pearls from fresh water clams, and ornaments of copper, silver, and gold. Some early explorers accepted his account about Norumbega, and the name began to appear on maps as early as 1574. Just as the existence of a city requires that its name appear on our maps, the appearance of a name on a map is proof to many that a city must exist there. There is no evidence today that Ingram's city really existed. (Although not shown on most Maine maps, you can visit a real Norumbega by driving south from Brooksville, which is on the coast of Maine near the mouth of the Penobscot River.)

No mystery surrounds Bangor's encounter with the Brady Gang. Al Brady and his two gang members, Clarence Shaffer and James Dalhover, were captured in Ohio after a bank holdup. On Columbus Day in 1936, they murdered a guard and escaped. Their criminal career for the next year took them through a dozen states, scores of robberies, at least four murders, and another jailbreak. After the death of John Dillinger, J. Edgar Hoover listed the Brady Gang as Public Enemy number one.

The law began to close in behind them. The Brady Gang chose Bangor as a safe haven. For their hideout Al Brady selected the Auto Rest Park in nearby Carmel because it had a skating rink, and Al loved to roller-skate. They rearmed themselves at Dakin's Sporting Goods Store on Central Street in downtown Bangor, purchasing two automatic pistols and a third one a few days later. Dalhover, Brady's front man, then asked about buying a submachine gun. (Ridiculed as sheer stupidity later, Brady might have believed that with the repeal of Prohibition, local rum runners would want to quietly dispose of weapons they no longer needed.) Assuming they were not going to hunt deer, the clerk said he could probably get one but it would take about a week. They left. He notified the police. They called in the FBI.

Dalhover was identified from photos as a member of the Brady Gang, and a deadly trap was set. Local police, shunted into minor roles, were annoyed but ignored. On October 12, 1937, the Brady Gang showed up to collect their submachine gun. Instead they collected gunfire. Watching from the street outside Dakin's, Shaffer saw an FBI agent arresting Dalhover inside. Shaffer fired through the window, wounding the agent. FBI agents waiting across the street and on rooftops immediately opened fire, and for about thirty seconds bullets flew everywhere. The street had not been closed off to pedestrians after the Brady Gang arrived. Miraculously, no pedestrians were injured, although a bullet just missed the thigh of a woman headed to work at a local department store.

Both Brady and Shaffer were shot dead in the street. Their sedan still had Ohio license plates, although scattered among the weapons on the backseat were a number of stolen plates. Dalhover was returned to Illinois and later executed for an earlier murder there. Shaffer's body was shipped to Illinois. Brady was buried in an unmarked grave in Bangor's Public Grounds Cemetery. His death certificate lists his occupation as "bandit." A polished, engraved granite tablet is embedded in the sidewalk where Brady and Shaffer died. It reads: NEAR THIS SPOT AL BRADY, PUBLIC ENEMY NO. 1, WAS SHOT AND KILLED BY FBI AGENTS ON OCT. 12, 1937.

It had been exactly one year since the trio broke out of jail in Ohio.

Travelers with time on their hands might want to use Bangor as a base for a quick side trip farther north. Gulf Hagas is up at Brownville Junction. Justifiably billed as "The Grand Canyon of the East," this scenic three-mile canyon has five major waterfalls. The sidewalls are nearly vertical and rise up forty yards. The total hydraulic drop is 125 yards. Looking at it today, imagine what it looked like in the days when logs were being driven through this gorge. (Just west of the gorge and eighteen miles north of Dover is Greeley's Landing, which is the exact geographic center of Maine.)

Traveling from Bangor to Calais (pronounced CAL-iss), one can take either the high road or the low road. The main high road is I-95 heading north, but if you use U.S. 2 instead, you will pass through the town of Lincoln. In land area it's the largest town east of the Mississippi River. Local historians there can direct you to a rather odd but warmly human gravestone. The epitaph reads:

> *Sacred to the Memory of Mr. Jared Bates who Died Aug. the 6th, 1800. His Widow aged 24 who mourns as one who can be comforted lives at 7 Elm street this village and possesses every qualification for a good Wife.*

At Mattawamkeag, you can use Route 157 to get back on I-95.

About thirty miles farther north is Patten and the Lumberman's Museum, located on Shin Pond Road just west of the town. For more than 160 years, thousands of woodsmen, horses, and supplies passed over Shin Pond Road heading up-country to cut lumber in northern Maine. The Lumberman's Museum is a graphic record of that lumber industry. Its collections are housed in ten buildings, one of which is the 1820 logging camp, an exact reproduction of early camps and fully equipped with tools and utensils. Such camps housed twelve to fourteen men, who used an ox team to haul logs. The oddity in this camp is that not a single nail was used in its construction. See for yourself.

I-95 ends at the Canadian border in the town of Houlton. Stop long enough to look at an unusual fountain in Pierce Park. There are eight drinking fountains around the edge and two troughs close to the ground for small animals. Standing on a rock in the middle of a pool is the statue of a boy holding a leaky boot out of which water pours. The fountain was constructed in 1916 and the statue ordered from a catalog. Who created the statue? Its sculptor and national origin are unknown even though twenty-five somewhat similar statues can be seen in Europe and the United States. No one knows what the statue symbolizes. Is the boy trying to put out a fire? Is he carrying water to a wounded soldier in the only utensil he could find? Or has he simply discovered that his worn boot

Leaky boot fountain

needs repair? Join the many other people who photograph the fountain each year and then sample the cool, fresh drinking water before heading south to Calais on U.S. 1, an unusual highway that stretches all the way from northern Maine to Key West, Florida.

If you decided to skip the high road at Bangor and take the low road instead, you would be heading east on Route 9, named the Airline Road in 1857. It follows a wilderness road used to speed militia to the Canadian border from Bangor. Back then the coastal road took two days to travel and the wilderness route cut that time in half. It became so popular for travelers that business declined along the shore route. Owners there started the rumor that hungry wolves harassed travelers on the Airline Road. The rumor backfired as increasing numbers of hunters and adventurous travelers booked passage along the Airline, hoping to encounter some excitement. For a brief period the road was known as the Wolf Route.

At the end of the road, Calais is Maine's only city on the state's long border with Canada. Drinking water comes from Canada's sister city across the boundary. Fire engines, ambulances, and squad cars in both cities answer calls from either one and national holidays are mutually celebrated. But curious tourists reaching Calais soon become mired in conflicting claims about the easternmost locations in our nation. Lubec claims to be the easternmost town. Eastport says it is the most easterly city and the West Quoddy Head lighthouse station argues that it is the easternmost point. Really doesn't make that much difference. Somewhere around here is where the rising sun casts its first rays on the continental United States. The popular belief is that West Quoddy Head gets the first rays but that seems to be true only from March 7 to March 24 and from September 19 to October 6. For most of the year the winner is little-known Mars Hill, 1,660 feet high and on the New Brunswick line north of Maine's Washington County. (According to the International Dateline, the U.S. city where each day begins first is apparently Agana in Guam.)

Heading south toward Eastport there is a small pull-off picnic area on the right in Perry. Inscribed on a red granite stone is: THIS STONE MARKS LATITUDE 45° NORTH HALFWAY FROM THE EQUATOR TO THE POLE. 1896. The boulder rests on a line that circles the globe, passing eventually through southern France, northern Italy, Russia, Turkestan, Mongolia, and northern Japan, and entering the United States again midway between Portland and Salem, Oregon.

Eastport is where you go to see the Old Sow. Usually viewed from a safe distance, the adventurous traveler can get a closer look if a skipper willing to take the risk can be found. Some atlases list the Old Sow as the largest whirlpool in the world while others claim it is merely the largest in the western hemisphere. Eastport is willing to settle for the more modest title.

A homegrown whirlpool is what you see while water is draining out of the kitchen sink. Because it is controlled solely by the earth's rotation, it spins one way in the northern hemisphere and the opposite way in the southern. To be a true whirlpool, however, the spinning vortex must be caused by multiple, colliding, tidal currents. The ocean floor under the Old Sow is about 220 feet down and is surrounded by holes much deeper. An incoming tide converges from two directions at high speed, ramming the sea upward in a swirling motion. Hundreds of smaller whirlpools are usually visible. Because of the sucking sounds they emit, these are the "little piglets" that gave the whirlpool its name. Some boats have had close encounters with the Old Sow. It has tipped over a tanker and chewed many smaller craft to bits. (One fisherman resented having to force his boat *uphill* in order to escape.) The Old Sow can be seen from the shore at Eastport, but take the ferry to Deer Island for a closer look. If you are persuasive and the tide is right, the ferry captain has been known to steer a course fairly close to the vortex. The best time to view its action is about two hours before or after high water during the spring tides.

The Old Sow is not Eastport's only odd attraction. Dotting the coves and bays around it are the salmon pens, linked together in long chains, in which millions of salmon and trout are reared, making Eastport the "salmonid aquaculture capital of North America." In nearby West Pembroke are the little-known but fantastic Reversing Falls. Through a three hundred–yard gap, a tidal flow alternately fills and empties two bays. Water moving at a speed of twenty-five knots over jutting rocks causes the "falls." Later, as the direction of water changes, new ripples in the opposite direction appear and the six-hour-long roar of the falls begins again. Arrive with a picnic lunch one hour before high water. Munch and watch while the direction of the falls changes during the next two hours.

Much of Maine's history is located along the coastal route westward from Eastport. A field of needlelike spires juts into the sky at Cutler, where the U.S. Naval Computer and Telecommunications Station operates the world's most powerful radio transmitter. There are twenty-six antenna masts capable of withstanding winds of 150 knots. Ranging in height from 800 to 980 feet, some are taller than the Bunker Hill and Washington monuments placed one on top of the other. The antenna wires are counterweighted to compensate for excess sagging during icy conditions. This U.S. Navy base provides radio communication to all units of the U.S. fleet in the North Atlantic, Europe, and the Arctic.

In nearby Machias, anyone pausing long enough to admire the town's beauty will learn by then that the first naval engagement of the Revolutionary War took place there. By June of 1775 the British were pumping up their troop strength in Boston, and Machias was ordered to supply lumber for the additional barracks. Machias citizens debated the issue alongside a small stream just east of the O'Brien Cemetery. Benjamin Foster, objecting to the British demand, jumped across the stream and urged those who agreed to do likewise. Eventually everyone did so. That spot is now known as "Foster's Rubicon," named after Julius Caesar's crossing of the Rubicon River against government orders and thereby changing the course of history. (While the exact location of Caesar's Rubicon is still debatable, we are able to be more precise!)

To enforce its order, the British had sent the heavily armed *Margaretta* to Machias. Using lumber sloops and armed only with muskets, swords, pitchforks, and axes, the rebels in Machias attacked the British man-of-war five days before the Bunker Hill battle. In capturing the ship, American patriots had won their first naval victory.

Almost hidden within the annals of this incident is the heroic action of two women in Jonesboro, sixteen miles through dense forests from Machias. Answering the patriotic call from Machias, Jonesboro men set out to hew a path there. Hannah Weston realized that the ammunition they carried was too limited to be useful. Collecting all of the powder, lead, and pewter she could find in the village, Hannah, who was only seventeen, and her sister-in-law Rebecca, nineteen, labored through that wilderness from Jonesboro to Machias, each carrying a load of thirty to forty pounds.

Hannah Weston was the great-granddaughter of Hannah Dustin, another New England heroine, who has her own memorial in Boscawen, New Hampshire, (see pages 48–49). Hannah Weston is buried in a small family cemetery plot in Jonesboro. The burial plot is visible from the town offices there and information about how to reach it is available. Her grave is worth a visit.

The waters off Machias were plagued by pirates. Requirements that colonists purchase only high-priced goods from the mother country encouraged smuggling, and so privateers began seizing ship cargoes. Pirate Sam Bellamy had a talent for converting captured crews into pirates. In the early 1700s this "Robin Hood of the High Seas" forced captives to build a fort at Machias, where he intended to set up a pirate's utopia. He then made one last trip to finance his retirement. After failing to vanquish a French vessel, Bellamy captured a New Bedford whaler. As usual, he offered to let its crew join his gang; apparently they agreed, and their captain volunteered to lead the way through treacherous reefs along the coast. When Bellamy's boat followed his lead, the captain grounded his own vessel and watched as the pirate ship smashed itself on the rocks, drowning Bellamy and most of his crew. "Robin Hood" should never have crossed swords with a whaling captain!

Sooner or later, almost everyone visits Bar Harbor. Much has been written about its beauty and the many pleasures it offers. However, it has one oddity that seldom gets mentioned. Located in the shadow of Cadillac Cliffs is Thunder Hole, a tidal cavern carved out by wave action. Thunder Hole gets its name from the sounds it makes about three hours before high tide. Waves trapped in the cave create noises that boom like thunder. Water spouts as high as forty feet are common.

The road between Bar Harbor and Castine is anything but straight. The area is worth a visit because of what happened here to the Revolutionary War hero Paul Revere. Our most familiar image of him has been formed by Longfellow's poem *Paul Revere's Ride*. His military record during the war is seldom mentioned. At Castine, Revere had his great moment in battle—which ended in his court-martial.

Paul Revere longed for the glory of a real military exploit—until 1779, when he got his chance and lost. At Castine the British had begun building a new fort not far from their stronghold, Fort George. Massachusetts patriots countered by dispatching to the area an impressive naval armada and a much less impressive scraped-together army of soldiers, including Lt. Col. Paul Revere, who was in charge of artillery. On July 28 the soldiers scrambled ashore in the largest amphibious operation of the war. The British backed away from their unfinished fort and dug in. Thinking they would be overwhelmed, their commanding officer planned to fire a few token rounds and then surrender. The Yankees never attacked.

Fort George was the target and the problem. Army commanders believed the fort could not be taken without a navy barrage, but navy commanders refused to risk their vessels that close to the fort. It was a standoff in a divided command. When the order to "attack without delay" finally came from Massachusetts, it was too late. A British relief squadron had moved in and the Penobscot expedition erupted into an ignominious, chaotic scramble for safety. The American fleet grounded itself, destroyed its ships and equipment, and headed for the hills. The militiamen were left to get home as best they could. During the panic, Revere lost contact with his artillerymen. With the one vessel assigned to him, he tried desperately to find them. The Yankee second-in-command, Gen. Peleg Wadsworth, demanded that Revere use his vessel for a different purpose, but Revere refused.

When it was time to fix the blame, Revere was the obvious scapegoat. On September 9, a special committee began to investigate the disaster. The most damaging testimony against Revere came from General Wadsworth's bitter criticism. Revere defended himself on the grounds that since the siege had ended and the expedition had failed, he was no longer required to obey the instructions he got from his superiors. Revere was censured for misconduct. He was neither condemned nor acquitted.

Revere demanded a full court-martial so he could clear his name. After many refusals and three years after the botched expedition, a court was convened in February 1782. Only the two charges for which he had earlier been censured were considered. The court acquitted him on both. Though finally cleared of all blame for the Penobscot fiasco, Revere found that the decision did little to remove the tarnish from his reputation. He resumed his career as a silversmith.

Seventy-nine years later, the tarnish suddenly disappeared. In 1861 Longfellow published his poem *Paul Revere's Ride*. Intended to stimulate enlistment in the Union Army, Longfellow portrayed Paul Revere as the ideal patriot answering his nation's call. The stirring verses transformed Paul Revere from a minor participant in the revolution into an immortal American hero. In one of life's more delicious ironies, Gen. Peleg Wadsworth was indirectly responsible for helping Paul Revere to become that hero. After all, it was his grandson, Henry Wadsworth Longfellow, who wrote the poem.

Circling down the west side of Penobscot Bay on U.S. 1, pause in Camden, where the mountains meet the sea. (Anyone doubting the validity of that slogan should drive to the top of nearby Mount Battie.) Just beyond Camden is Rockport, where "the Spite House" is now located out on Deadman Point. Actually built in Phippsburg, eighty-five miles away, it was intended to be more magnificent than the mansion James McCobb had built for his second wife. Already the father of a son and daughter before his third marriage, James died while his son, Thomas, was at sea. Before Thomas returned, the third Mrs. McCobb had arranged a wedding between her son by an earlier marriage and Thomas's sister, putting Mrs. McCobb in control of one of the area's largest and loveliest estates. When Thomas returned and learned what she had done, he was furious. He swore he would build a mansion beautiful enough and large enough to overshadow his stepmother's inherited residence. In 1806 he made good on his promise. From the day it was completed, it has been known as "the Spite House." In 1925 its owner moved it, partly overland and partly by barge, to its current location.

Just south of Rockport is the small town of Glen Cove, which has the unique honor of being the birthplace of Capt. Hanson Gregory. While not yet twenty he became one of Maine's youngest sea captains and had already been decorated by Spain's Queen Isabella for saving the lives of an entire shipwrecked Spanish crew. But his real claim to fame was his invention of what we now call the doughnut, as commemorated by a plaque in front of his birthplace in Glen Cove. He didn't actually invent the doughnut itself. What Captain Gregory really invented was the doughnut *hole*. While still in Holland, the pilgrims had learned how to make the Dutch "oil cake," a small ball about the size of a walnut made from sweetened dough and fried in deep fat, which usually left a soggy center. In removing the middle, Captain Gregory showed that it is possible to improve on something by adding "nothing" to it.

There are at least two versions about how Captain Gregory made his discovery. One claims that in 1847 he poked holes in his mother's doughnuts to eliminate those soggy centers and allow for more uniform frying. The more popular (and colorful) version has Captain Gregory, partial to doughnuts, growing fond of midmorning snacks for himself and the crew. During one turbulent passage, he discovered he could manage the ship's wheel and still hang on to his doughnut if he spiked it on one of the wheel's spokes. He could have his cake and eat it too! In November of 1941 a debate about which version was true took place in New York's Astor Hotel. The judges (literary luminaries Clifton Fadiman, Elsa Maxwell, and Franklin P. Adams) unanimously favored his mother's kitchen. Their decision was ratified forty years later by the Smithsonian Institution. (A third theory holds that the hole in the doughnut was "invented" by the Pennsylvania Dutch. But they didn't live in Glen Cove.)

Thomaston is at the head of the Saint George River, just west of Rockland. At the river's mouth is Allen Island, where Capt. George Weymouth planted a cross in 1605, making the first known claim of possession by an Englishman on New England soil. The house at 25 Main Street in Thomaston is where Congressman Jonathan Cilley lived until he lost a gun duel in February 1838. Elected to Congress in 1836, Cilley found fertile soil to indulge his zest for political warfare. Southerners still took the dueling code seriously, often taunting the less warlike northerners. Cilley disdained their intimidation tactics. After one rancorous floor debate, an obscure congressman from Kentucky named William Graves was persuaded to hand Cilley a note demanding clarification of his remarks. Cilley refused. A second note was delivered requesting "that satisfaction which is recognized among gentlemen." Feeling that his honor (and New England's) was at stake, Cilley accepted the challenge and chose rifles at eighty yards as the weapon. At the command "Fire!" Cilley discharged his weapon into the ground. Graves fired and missed. Graves refused to allow the matter to rest and a second exchange took place. This time Graves accidentally discharged his rifle and Cilley's shot barely missed Graves. Incredibly, a third exchange was agreed to and Cilley became the first and only incumbent New England congressman to be slain in a duel.

Maine's only military execution took place at Thomaston. The British were dug in upriver at Castine and the waters were full of Tory privateers roaming the coast, attacking shipping and conducting raids ashore. Responsibility for protecting Maine with a few hundred men went to Gen. Peleg Wadsworth (who remained untarnished by his part in the Penobscot blunders). To dampen loyalist activity and isolate the British, he declared martial law and drew a line beyond which no American vessel could sail. Under martial law, those of doubtful loyalty could be tried by the military and could be sentenced to death—but it didn't solve the problem. A patriot was killed, his wife injured, and their home looted. Wadsworth publicly announced that he would execute the next person convicted of aiding the enemy. That happened to be a rather dull-witted person named Jeremiah Braun, whose actions may have been stupid but not malicious. A pardon was requested by many who believed his sentence was only a feint to prevent other offenses, but General Wadsworth was adamant. The culprit was hanged on Limestone Hill. Despite public disapproval, General Wadsworth felt his harshness was proper and useful. Eventually, public disapproval of martial law resulted in a reversal of Wadsworth's methods. Limestone Hill is now the site of the Maine State Prison. If you're not interested in the place where Braun was hung, it's still worth a visit because the prison has a showroom where some unusual handcrafted items created by prisoners can be purchased.

In the brief age of the clipper ships, the *Red Jacket* was known as "the fastest ship afloat." It was launched from a Rockland shipyard in 1853. Manned by an indifferent crew, she set sail for England on January 11, 1854, in rainy and unpleasant weather. Pelted at times with rain, snow, hail, heavy seas, and shifting winds that blew her off course, the *Red Jacket* plowed on toward England as best she could. When the ship arrived at the Mersey River on January 23, the weather was so bad there wasn't a willing river pilot to be found. Capt. Asa Eldridge was not deterred. He took the *Red Jacket* up the river "with every stitch of canvas drawing in the brisk northwest wind" and came up alongside the pier head with a flourish. The journey from New York to Liverpool took thirteen days, one hour, and twenty-five minutes, dock to dock. On her maiden voyage the *Red Jacket* established a record that still stands for any ship under sail. Unfortunately, there seems to be no monument or marker about it in Rockland.

West of the Rockland area in Muscongus Bay is Loud's Island. Its earlier name was Muscongus Island. For many years the islanders considered themselves to be part of the nearby town of Bristol. Technically the island didn't belong to Bristol—it didn't even belong to Maine, since an early geodetic survey of Maine's coast omitted any mention of the island. But that didn't upset anybody. The Bristol tax collector rowed over, chalked on each house the amount of taxes due, and after the money had been paid, officially erased that figure.

It worked out real friendly until the national elections in 1860. Most people in Bristol voted Republican, but everyone on Loud's Island was a Democrat. When the votes were counted, the Democrats had edged out the Republicans. Bristol was enraged. Someone recalled that Loud's Island didn't really belong to Bristol. The islanders' votes were tossed out and Bristol became a Republican victory. So the islanders seceded from Bristol, pledging that they would govern themselves as the Republic of Muscongus. Bristol didn't take the resolution seriously until their tax collector arrived on the island. As rapidly as he chalked figures, the islanders erased them. "No votes, no taxes!" The new republic was willing to support the United States but not the town of Bristol.

Bristol continued to ignore the republic until 1863, when nine men from the island were drawn in the town's draft for Civil War soldiers. When recruiting officers rowed over to gather the recruits, they were met at the waterfront by every man and boy on the island—all armed. The officers returned to the mainland without the recruits. (Later, one officer went back to try again. At his first house call, the housewife was busy peeling potatoes. When she learned of his mission, she pelted him with whatever was in reach, including potatoes and peelings. He abandoned his mission and reported, "If I had a regiment of women like her, I'd take Richmond inside of three days!") To make their patriotism clear, each of the draftees paid the legal sum of three hundred dollars to buy a mainland substitute to serve for them instead. Another nine hundred dollars was raised and given to the federal government to "help lick the rebels." It wasn't until 1934 that the Republic of Muscongus petitioned for readmission to the United States.

Damariscotta is just off of U.S. 1, near Newcastle. The area abounds with familiar names like Jefferson, Walpole, Newcastle, and Bunker Hill, and some not so familiar, such as Duckpuddle, Dutch Neck, and Oyster Creek. Oysters, incidentally, are Damariscotta's major oddity. Banked up along the Damariscotta River are mounds of shining white oyster shells, some of which are six thousand years old. (Archaeologists call such mounds "middens," but the locals just call them "shell heaps.") Shells are piled up on both sides of the river below the south side of the bridge. Those on the western shore (the Glidden Midden) are now more visible than those on the eastern shore (the Whaleback Midden). More than a million cubic feet of shells have been piled up over three acres. In 1886 the largest heap was 341 feet long by 126 feet wide and from 4 to 20 feet high. It has been estimated that the original oyster lovers must have eaten 35 million bushels to have created the heaps. Some of the shells were twelve to fourteen inches long and three to four inches wide. Burial grounds at the edge of the heaps held skeletons sitting upright and facing the rising sun.

The efforts of archaeologists have been somewhat hampered because hundreds of tons of shells were mined as a source of lime for a local limestone factory. Erosion played its part. Still, we know that over the centuries, the shell heaps have built up into three distinct layers. The bottom layer was probably created by prehistoric peoples feasting there. Because that layer contains evidence of mollusks that favor warmer waters, it's likely that geologic evolution was taking place. The middle layer contains traces left by the Red Paint People, so named because each grave discovered of that period contained a significant quantity of brilliant red ocher. The upper layer is evidently the accumulation from more recent oyster orgies by Indian tribes. The Skidompha Library in Damariscotta can supply travelers with detailed information.

U.S. 1 leads westward to Wiscasset, a town with distinctive charm. Those traveling through the town center pass a corner that, unknown to them, contains a unique oddity. In the small park opposite the post office is a sunken garden, easily unseen since it lies below ground level. The site was originally the cellar of the Whittier (pronounced WHICH-er) Tavern, a rather large house with a huge central chimney. It was possible to sit within the fireplace and look up at the stars. Ebenezer Whittier was the innkeeper and the only one in town licensed to sell rum. The tavern burned in 1843 and his son-in-law, Ebenezer Hilton, built a new hotel on the site. (It was the first Hilton hotel in Maine and perhaps the first anywhere.) That building burned down in 1903 and the Sortwell family, who lived across the street, bought the property. They cleared the rubble and hired an eminent landscape architect, Wolcott Andrews, to design a garden using the old cellar hole and the surrounding lawns. He created a beautiful spot with a variety of plants that blossom from early spring until the autumn frosts. The sunken garden has been deeded to the town of Wiscasset and is maintained by a special committee. Occasionally used for wedding ceremonies, the town will gladly share the beauty of its sunken garden with anyone passing by.

Collectors of architectural oddities might enjoy a side trip by following Route 27 north from Wiscasset and turning westward at Randolph to West Gardiner. The Jesse Tucker House is on Hallowell Road. It's an octagonal structure built in 1856. The theory of an octagonal house was conceived by Orson Fowler eight years earlier and went on to achieve some minor popularity with builders. There are at least fifteen such houses in Maine. Fowler believed that an octagonal shape produced one-fifth more livable space in it than would a square shape with the same circumference. It would make for better heating and a more compact internal floor plan, saving a vast number of housekeeping steps. Besides, he claimed, "It has greater beauty because it approaches more closely the sphere, the predominant form of nature." What makes the Jesse Tucker House unique is not only its shape but its construction. Though no longer apparent from the outside, the outer walls were constructed of ten-inch-wide wooden slabs, each about an inch thick. Instead of placing them upright, the boards were layered horizontally, flat side to flat side. Piled up one on top of the other, they were stacked to a three-story height to form the walls of the building. Now, that's unusual!

Another octagonal structure can be found down the road apiece at Poland Spring, just beyond Lewiston. (Take I-495 south and exit toward Danville, then follow Route 122 westward to Poland Spring.) Maine chose the octagon form for its State Pavilion at the Columbian Exposition in Chicago at the end of the nineteenth century. The design may have been influenced by the small, irregularly shaped lot assigned to Maine, but an octagon was the solution. When the exhibition closed, the building was purchased by Hiram Ricker and Sons, disassembled, and moved by freight train and finally by horse and wagon to Poland Spring. Poland Spring is a resort area and the reassembled edifice became the Maine State Building, serving as library, museum, and art gallery to the many guests there.

Though long a resort area, Poland Spring is best known today as the source of Poland Spring mineral water. In 1880 Joseph Ricker, "at death's door and not to last the night, drank freely of the springwater brought to him by his nurse, and lived another fifty-two years." By 1910 Poland Spring water was being sold in Central and South America, and booklets about it were published in Spanish. Carloads of it were sent free to San Francisco after the 1906 earthquake. In the Maine State Building you can see what is probably the world's largest collection of an unusual Poland Spring artifact, the "Moses bottle." Made of molded glass, each bottle depicts a seated man with a long beard wearing what appears to be a sleeved robe and holding a canelike staff propped upright between his knees. No one seems to know the reason why he is thought to look like Moses. Perhaps it's the biblical appearance of the beard. However, the Moses symbol was chosen by Poland Spring because of "the story of his smiting the rock with a rod and water coming forth."

The Moses bottle made its first appearance in 1876. Ordered for the grand opening of the Poland Spring Hotel in 1876, the bottles were filled with Poland Spring water and given away as souvenirs. Over the years there have been about forty variants of the Moses bottle. In the Philadelphia area the bottle was affectionately referred to as "old Mister Whiskers." Sometimes clear, aqua, or deep olive in color, the emerald green bottle was the real favorite. In 1931 one was given to all honeymoon guests at Poland Spring. A sign attached to the bottles said, "A baby guaranteed with every bottle." Often they were refilled at the spring by couples who carried the water away with them.

Some consider Gray, south of Poland Spring on Route 26, to be the crossroads of Maine because six major routes pass through the village. Travelers interested in oddities should pause there because Gray has an intriguing oddity. A southern soldier from the Civil War is buried there, and nobody knows who he is. In the Gray Village Cemetery is a gravestone simply inscribed, "Stranger, a soldier of the late war, died 1862." After Lt. Charles Colley of the Tenth Maine Volunteers was killed in the Battle of Cedar Mountain, Colley's family arranged for his body to be returned to Gray. When the casket arrived it contained the body of an unidentified Confederate soldier. The War Department was unable to explain the error. A group of local women in Gray arranged with the town fathers and Gray residents to buy a plot in the cemetery. The town offered to pay for the stone and the appropriate inscription. The unknown Confederate soldier was buried. This unusual event later received some publicity. So many Confederate flags were sent to Gray to be used at the grave site that the town still has an ample supply. On Memorial Day every year, two flags decorate the site, one the Stars and Stripes and the other the Stars and Bars. (Lieutenant Colley's body was found and shipped to Gray a few weeks later. He is buried not far from the final resting place of "the stranger.")

Freeport is located on the coast west of Gray. Anyone seriously planning to head out into the wilds probably has spent some time shopping at L. L. Bean. It is open twenty-four hours every day to sell all manner of wilderness outfitting, from clothing to canoes. Freeport has two oddities. Both are readily visible, but both deserve some advance mention. Atop a massive concrete slab, the forty-foot *Big Indian* statue is located a mile north of I-95's exit 17. Brainchild of a local merchant who sold moccasins, the *Big Indian* wears a brightly colored pair. While on a flatbed trailer en route to Freeport from Pennsylvania, where it was crafted, the statue reportedly caused the biggest traffic jam in the history of the New Jersey Turnpike. Rubbernecks in cars pulling abreast slowed so their startled passengers could stare, point fingers, crank down windows, and reach for cameras. Cars piled up behind them and they also slowed down. Turnpike authorities finally pulled the trailer off the road until nightfall, when it was allowed to continue under cover of darkness.

Freeport's other oddity is probably mentioned in every Maine guidebook. Maine has a desert! I don't mean Mount Desert Island, but a real desert, just like the Gobi and the Sahara. Believe it or not, it is simply called the Desert of Maine. It's a perfect specimen of what happens when humans and nature collide. About eight thousand years ago a glacier slid past this area, leaving behind a large sand deposit. With the passage of much time, the sea of sand became covered with earth and vegetation and it looked much like the landscape around it. And then in 1797 the Tuttle family established their three hundred–acre farm above the sea of sand. For several years they grew healthy crops, but failure to rotate crops, combined with overgrazing and massive land clearing, slowly eroded the thin skin above the sand. Gradually the sand appeared and seemed to spread as its protective covering disappeared. It has climbed over and buried buildings, throwing up dunes as high as seventy feet. It now covers more than one hundred acres and continues to grow.

South of Freeport is Portland, the largest city in Maine, with a record for vitality and action. It is a peninsula that has been known by a number of names, including Falmouth. Three times it has risen from its own ashes. Indians devastated it, the British burned it, and in 1866 a great fire consumed it. Each time Portland rebuilt. Portland was once almost destroyed by riots. Three times in a little more than a year, violence broke out against "a nest of little, mean, filthy boxes of that description commonly called houses of ill-fame, tenanted by the most loathsome and vicious of the human species, and made a common resort for drunken sailors and the lowest off-scouring of society." (Now that's what I call an articulate put-down!) These were Portland's Whorehouse Riots in 1825, in which the destruction of brothels culminated in gunfire.

A happier event produced an oddity down in Kennebunkport. (It's farther south on U.S. 1 and east of Kennebunk itself). Although a private residence, passersby can still enjoy the Victorian beauty of the Wedding Cake House. Built by a sea captain for his bride, explanations for its unusual architecture differ. Some say it was simply a reminder of their wedding cake; others believe it was designed as a substitute for the cake she never got because he was hastily called out to sea in an emergency. Other stories include a new bride committing suicide by throwing herself down the stairs, several ghosts, and a few murders. The probable truth is that the builder originally constructed a simpler house but because he loved to carve, he later adorned it with lots of elaborate wooden fretwork. The outside of the house looks as though it was created with a scroll saw. Elaborate pinnacles rise above the roofline. Connecting them horizontally at the top of the first and second floors are traceries that look like delicate lace. The total effect is thoroughly enchanting (but please don't trespass).

York is about as far south as you can go in Maine. Once a popular summer playground for Indians, York was chartered in 1641, making it the oldest chartered city in America. York's Old Town Gaol is the oldest existing English public building in America. Built to house provincial prisoners in 1653, the gaol was also a silent threat to Royalists. It continued to function as a prison until 1860. In 1692 the Candlemass Massacre took place at York. Violating a treaty they had signed in 1691, five hundred Abenaki Indians raided the village, killing forty-eight colonists, capturing another seventy, and torching the town. Five miles north on Chases Pond Road is Snowshoe Rock, where the Abenakis stacked their snowshoes before the attack. A plaque commemorates the event. Four-year-old Jeremiah Moulton was forced to watch as his parents were scalped before his eyes. Jeremiah got his revenge a full thirty-two years later when he led the raid that wiped out the Indians at Norridgewock. As they say in Maine, what goes around, comes around.

A final oddity about Maine: it's the only state in America with a name that has just one syllable.

MASSACHUSETTS

The best place to begin a tour through Massachusetts is where the Pilgrims began theirs in 1620. They landed at the outer tip of Cape Cod, a place we now call Provincetown. Although they weren't called Pilgrims until many years later, there's a 252-foot Pilgrim Memorial Monument at Provincetown, believed to be the tallest granite structure in the United States. From its top, you can look down on the harbor and beach and imagine for yourself how it all began when the solitary *Mayflower* dropped anchor somewhere out there in the bay. The site of their first landfall is marked by a tablet on a low granite slab at the juncture of Commercial Street and Beach Highway. No Plymouth Rock here. Their small landing craft was a shallop, a sort of big rowboat with a mast and sails and oars for eight men. Like most explorers reaching land, they stepped out of their small boat and simply waded ashore. If you happen to be in Provincetown at sunset, go out to Race Point. It's the only place in New England where you can watch as the sun goes down into the Atlantic Ocean at sunset.

There's only one way to leave Provincetown by car, and that's "down," meaning south on U.S. 6. Truro is along the way, but before you get there look for Corn Hill Road, because a plaque set in stone in the Corn Hill parking area says, SIXTEEN PILGRIMS LED BY MYLES STANDISH, WILLIAM BRADFORD, STEPHEN HOPKINS AND EDWARD TILLEY FOUND THE PRECIOUS INDIAN CORN ON THIS SPOT, WHICH THEY CALLED CORN HILL. NOVEMBER 16, 1620. The small scouting party noticed curious heaps of sand in a meadow near the shore. Digging into one, they uncovered a large basket containing three or four bushels of corn. They took as much as they could carry and buried the remainder. Returning to the site about ten days later, they dug up the rest of the corn and some additional corn discovered at other sites in the area. Altogether they stole about ten bushels of corn from the Indians. When planted, this seed corn provided just enough food for the Pilgrims to survive through the next winter. No one knows what happened to the Indians who were presumably storing it for the same purpose.

An unusual landmark is easily seen on Coast Guard Road in Truro, a fifty-five-foot tower that had for many years been part of the Fitchburg Railroad Depot in South Boston. When the depot was torn down in 1927, a Truro resident bought the tower and had it reconstructed in Truro as a memorial to his father. It has since come to be known as the Jenny Lind Tower. During one of the years it was in South Boston, Jenny Lind, the "Swedish nightingale," agreed to sing in a hall nearby in East Boston. Her popularity drew such a mob that when it was discovered that the promoters had oversold the tickets, loud and angry protests threatened Lind's performance. But she found a way to please everyone by singing to the entire mob from the top of the tower.

Tourists stopping at the Salt Pond Visitor Center just off U.S. 6 in Eastham have a rare opportunity to discover just what it is like to be totally blind. The Buttonbush Trail was specially designed as a self-guiding nature trail for blind persons to use but can be a learning experience for others who are willing to keep their eyes closed while moving along the trail. Buttonbush is a quarter-mile-loop trail with a guide rope and text panels in both Braille and large lettering. As users walk along, following the guide rope and stopping to "read" the text panels, they learn about the area's history and nature through touching, feeling, hearing, and smelling. A round float on the guide rope indicates the presence of a text panel. A smooth bump on the rope indicates a step up or down. In order to accommodate wheelchairs, the first portion of the trail is gently graded without any steps. The trail includes a foot bridge over a shallow pond filled with buttonbush shrubs. Designed to encourage multiple sensory experiences, the trail is popular with a wide variety of users. It may be the only public trail of its kind.

Orleans (pronounced or-LEENS), the only town on the Cape with a French name, is south of Truro and close to Cape Cod's "elbow." Orleans was shelled by a German submarine during World War I. Submarines were something new at the time, and our naval officials thought the East Coast was relatively safe because surface vessels could be spotted from a great distance, and it seemed submarines would not be a menace because the distance was too great for them to gamble on getting back to Germany if damaged. The German navy took the gamble. In an effort to force us to pull back some of the effective antisubmarine vessels we had stationed in the critical area west of the British Isles and France, six German subs crossed the Atlantic in 1918. One of these was the U-156. Sometimes using a false funnel to disguise herself as a steamer, the U-156 had already sunk three vessels before arriving off the coast of Orleans on July 21. The tug *Perth Amboy* was three miles out, hauling four barges, from Gloucester to New York, when the submarine opened fire. Surprised Orleans residents and summer visitors were drawn to the shore by the sound of guns. A shell set the tug afire, and within a couple of hours, the U-156 managed to sink all four barges, but only after approaching within a few hundred yards of them. Enemy shells began landing in Meeting House Pond, and the startled residents realized that their homes might be in danger. It was the first and only time during World War I that enemy shells landed on U.S. soil. What a collector's price those shells would bring today!

If you have time to gaze out over Meeting House Pond (which is really a tidal basin, near a spit of land known as Barley Neck), you might also visit the French Cable Museum, once the only underwater cable station in the United States. Before radio, telephone, television, and satellites, messages were sent and received in Morse code along an undersea cable laid along the floor of the Atlantic Ocean. The station began operation in 1890 as a direct communication link between France and New York, and was finally closed down in 1959. By then it had relayed messages about the sinking of the *Lusitania*, Lindbergh's successful landing in Paris, and, of course, the attack of the U-156 off Orleans.

U.S. 6 curves west at Harwich, a pleasing town named after one in England known to Queen Elizabeth as "Happy-go-lucky-Harwich." Its historical district was Cape Cod's first entry in the National Register of Historic Places. The Harwich Historical Society is housed in what was originally the first school of navigation in the United States.

There seem to be no plaques in honor of Enoch Crosby, born in Harwich in 1750. Enoch Crosby was the real-life model for James Fenimore Cooper's hero in his 1821 novel *The Spy*. Many critics consider *The Spy* to be one of his best works. In fact, it made his reputation, going through fifteen American printings before Cooper's death in 1851. Peddler Harvey Birch, hero of *The Spy*, is one of those "who has gone down to the tomb, stigmatized as a foe to the rights of his countrymen, while in secret he has been the useful agent of the Revolution."

Crosby's apprenticeship to a shoemaker ended when he turned twenty-one. Working as a journeyman in Danbury, he learned of the fight at Lexington. On his way to enlist, he happened to meet a stranger who thought Crosby was a British sympathizer and introduced him to many leaders in local Tory groups. Crosby later reported this to John Jay, who promptly recruited him to spy on the loyalists.

With a pack full of shoemaker's tools, Enoch Crosby traveled the countryside—once as far as Bennington, Vermont. Entering loyalist homes to repair old footwear or create new, he worked steadily and listened carefully. Soon after, loyalists gathering in some remote barn or lonely wood (or even an ingeniously hollowed-out haystack) were suddenly arrested. It took the loyalists a long time to surmise that Enoch Crosby was not really on their side. When they did, he suffered a severe beating. (Those who beat him were later hunted down as outlaws by the Whigs.) No longer anonymous, Crosby enlisted again in the army. In later years he led a peaceful life "without spot or blemish." In 1827 he was guest of honor at a New York performance of a play based on *The Spy*.

You won't need directions to find Hyannis, though it's not actually on U.S. 6. It's the largest village on the Cape. Amid the frenzied summer activity, the John F. Kennedy Memorial is touchingly simple in concept and worth a quiet moment. So is the Octagonal House on South Street, one of a number of eight-sided New England buildings that enjoyed an architectural vogue in the 1800s. Built in 1850 by Capt. Rodney Baxter, the eight concrete walls are eighteen inches thick, and it has two square rooms and a lot of smaller rooms with closets tucked into the oddly angled corners on each floor inside. (Sorry you can't see them—you can only admire the house from outside.)

Off the Cape's southern coast are the islands of Nantucket and Martha's Vineyard. Ferry service connects both with the mainland and with each other. Some of the ferries to Martha's Vineyard dock at Oak Bluffs. (Its original name in 1646 was "Easternmost Chop of Holmes' Hole," which qualifies as a kind of oddity itself.) Oak Bluffs has a very unique campground. Beginning in 1835 a grove of ancient oaks became the annual meeting place for members of the Methodist Church. At first there were tent gatherings for religious revivals, but as the congregation grew, permanent buildings appeared, now known as Cottage City. The centerpiece is a great conical open structure called the Tabernacle, built in 1897 with T-irons, angle irons, pipe, and wooden rafters supporting a corrugated roof. It is one of the largest wrought-iron structures in the United States and can seat two thousand people. Around it, in concentric circles, are three hundred tiny, colorful Victorian gingerbread cottages, ornately built with patterned shingles, decorative scrollwork moldings, turrets, spires, leaded glass windows, and wicker rockers on miniature porches with lacy railings. These "valentine houses" are so closely clustered—some less than two feet apart—that you'll wonder how anyone had enough room to swing a hammer while pounding shingle nails. The church continues to own the property on which the houses have been built. Illumination Night occurs in mid-August, presumably to mark the end of the summer season. Hundreds of Oriental lanterns are lit on the houses, the trees, and the winding streets. Cottage City becomes a fantastic fairyland. Now interdenominational, it is a haven for those wishing to escape from worldly stress. The architectural style developed there, dubbed "Carpenter Gothic," influenced other construction in Oak Bluffs, giving the whole village the appearance of a seaside toy shop.

As with any neighborhood containing family histories that are a century and a half old, Cottage City has its fair share of spectral spirits. In the front parlor of a cottage facing Sunset Lake, an invisible Chopin plays the piano. Unseen wraiths rap walls and move solid objects. In one cottage an elderly male ghost monopolizes the bathroom late at night. Imagine the inconvenience! For anyone interested in such phenomena, a local ghost tour is available.

There are two carousels in New England, each claiming to be the oldest in America. One (in Watch Hill, Rhode Island—see page 118) has horses that swing out as the carousel whirls. The carousel in Oak Bluffs is of the platform type with the horses going up and down. Strangely enough, both have the same name: the Flying Horses Carousel. The Oak Bluffs carousel was installed in 1884 in a large barnlike building. It was probably built between 1876–78 and may have been whirling around on Coney Island before being brought to Oak Bluffs. Children still reach for rings as they ride through space and time on their elegantly carved and painted steeds. In each horse's glass eye is a replica of a small animal.

Before heading back to the coast of Cape Cod Bay, you may want a side trip west on I-195 to stop in at Fall River, which has a number of oddities. A tablet at the corner of Fifth and Hartwell streets identifies the place where a skeleton dressed in armor was found in 1831. The discovery inspired Longfellow's poem "The Skeleton in Armor." Some of the unidentified remains can be viewed at the Fall River Historical Society. On the banks of the Quequechan River, there once stood a haunted hut occupied by an old crone believed to be a witch. Driven out and killed by superstitious neighbors, her hut was burned, but not before searchers found inside it a letter from Captain Kidd indicating that in earlier years she had been the famous pirate's mistress.

The Rolling Rock on Eastern Avenue facing Lafayette Park is balanced on a ledge. By applying force, the rock could be moved without rolling off the ledge. Local legend is that Indians used it to torture captives by rolling it over their arms, crushing flesh and bones.

Quite possibly the most famous spot in Fall River today is the house where Lizzie Borden lived—and where someone (was it Lizzie?) murdered her father and stepmother with an ax in August 1892 in their home, which still stands at 92 Second Street. The childhood rhyme that "Lizzie Borden took an ax and gave her mother forty whacks" claims she was guilty, but when tried for the murders, Lizzie was acquitted and the murders remain unsolved. Her trial produced one legal dialogue that still intrigues law students. The prosecution relied on the testimony of the maid, Bridget, to show animosity, anger, and emotional tension between members of the Borden family. But on cross-examination by the defense attorney, Bridget said that being called "Maggie" instead of "Bridget" was not unpleasant or offensive to her, that she had no trouble with anyone in the family, that the Borden residence was a pleasant place to live, and that she never saw "anything out of the way" or saw "any conflict in the family." After all, Bridget was a proper Irish maiden who would never publicly admit she had willingly served in an unwholesome household. Within the space of a few questions, Lizzie's defense attorney completely reversed Bridget's critical and key testimony. Perry Mason would have said, "Well done!"

The first duel in the New World took place on Plymouth's beach. Stephen Hopkins, a leader in the Plymouth Colony, had brought with him his daughter Constance and two servants, Edward Dotey and Edward Leister. Both were attracted to Constance and their competitive nature became violent. On the morning of June 18, 1621, they armed themselves with swords and daggers, left the Hopkins house, and found a deserted stretch of sand on the beach. During the subsequent duel, both were wounded, one in the hand, the other in the thigh. Their clashing swords awakened the colony. Governor Bradford decided that for punishment they were "to have their Head and Feet tied together, and so to lie for

24 hours without Meat or Drink." After an hour of this and upon promises of better behavior by the duelists and their master, they were released. Leister decided to seek his fortune elsewhere. "After he was at liberty, went to Virginia, & there dyed." Constance was married in Plymouth, but not to Dotey.

Most accounts of the War of 1812 focus on what happened in Baltimore, Washington, and New Orleans. Seldom noticed are minor battles and little skirmishes that also have their place in history. Farther north (along what is Route 3A today), an odd little skirmish occurred near the Scituate lighthouse on September 1, 1814. Having previously been threatened by a British man-of-war and heartened by its departure, the Scituate townspeople resumed their daily routines. Even the lighthouse keeper got busy gathering hay and apples, leaving his wife and children at the lighthouse. The two Bates girls, Rebecca, twenty-two, and Abigail, sixteen, polished the reflector and practiced "Yankee Doodle" on an old fife and a big drum. Suddenly their startled mother noticed the seventy-four-gun British warship *La Hogue* slipping out of the sea mist. The two Bates boys scuttled off to warn the town of its arrival. As the soldiers on the warship began climbing down into barges that would take them ashore, young Abigail had an idea about how they might help defend the town. Lugging the big drum and carefully carrying the cracked fife, the two girls crept unseen until they were hidden behind a large sand dune. Nodding in time, they began playing "Yankee Doodle." An off-shore wind carried the music out over the water. The sisters marched back and forth, still unseen but slowly approaching closer to the beach. Hidden from their sight, the first of the invasion barges came to a halt. Cheers arose from the village, shots were fired, and a second fife-and-drum band began sounding out "Yankee Doodle." On the motionless barges, the soldiers stared back at their ship. A signal flag and a puff of white smoke ordered them to return. They were in such a hurry to do so that three of the barges bumped into one another and one British soldier fell overboard. The derisive sound of "Yankee Doodle" pursued the British ship as it slowly sailed away. With their quick thinking and their musical talent, Abigail and Rebecca Bates had saved the town of Scituate.

Hingham, farther up the coast on Route 3A, has an old meeting house that is unique. The First Parish Meetinghouse on Main Street is commonly known as the "Old Ship Church," even though the Puritans who erected it never referred to the place where they worshiped as a church. The only example of medieval wooden craftsmanship on this continent, it is the oldest church in continual use in the United States and the oldest church building in New England. Architecturally, it stands alone. Instead of a cross or spire on a steeple, there is a functional tower with a bell and weather vane. It is called the Old Ship because it was built in 1681 by carpenters experienced in building ships and the angle braces (called "ship's knees") along with the curved roof timbers suggest the frame of an old wooden ship. Looking upward from the pews, the ceiling appears to be an upside-down ship's hull. Nearby trees were felled by parish members, who also used timbers from an earlier building. Subsequent years brought calamitous interior alterations, but eventually the people of Hingham demanded an authentic restoration of the original architecture and design. This was completed in 1930, making the Old Ship Church the best known and most admired structure in town.

One of the most popular persons in World War II was Kilroy. The phrase "Kilroy was here" was found inscribed on everything and everywhere, including airfields all over the world. Marines moving onto a beach, pilots landing on a remote airstrip, and soldiers attacking an enemy fortification frequently found that Kilroy had gotten there first. For many years his identity was a mystery, but when James J. Kilroy died in 1962, his legend did not. Kilroy began scrawling his phrase in Quincy, which is just up the coast outside of Boston. Two days before Pearl Harbor, Kilroy had gone to work at the Fore River Shipyard as an inspector. He placed a small check mark next to each rivet he inspected and later learned that because the riveters work was done piecemeal, some marks had been erased so that the riveter would receive additional credit from a later inspector. Kilroy immediately started writing KILROY WAS HERE with yellow chalk in large letters that could not be erased. Naval equipment began moving around the world. His slogan caught on and was soon being written by others in many odd places, and in much later times. When the first hydrogen bomb was exploded at Enewetak in the Pacific on November 6, 1952, scientists checking the guinea pig battleships used as targets found KILROY WAS HERE freshly painted on one of the hulls. In the late 1950s the following could be read on the wall of a frontier-type lodge on Alaska's Kenai Peninsula: HERE I STAND, FULL OF JOY. I GOT HERE BEFORE KILROY! Beneath it Kilroy had written: SORRY TO SPOIL YOUR LITTLE JOKE. I GOT HERE FIRST BUT MY PENCIL BROKE.

At last we get to Boston, where much of the state's history began. Wherever there's a lot of history, there are bound to be some oddities, and Boston has its share. Two can be found in a tourist attraction called the Freedom Trail. By following markers on the sidewalk, visitors can hike their way through history, standing on the very spot where famous events took place. Except for the Boston Massacre. Its memorial on the Freedom Trail is a raised circle of paving stones located in front of the Old State House. But that's not where the Boston Massacre took place. To stand on the real site, you have to walk about five hundred feet down State Street to the opening of Exchange Street opposite Quaker Lane. Back in 1770, a customs house stood at that intersection. On March 5 of that year, a single British soldier was on duty there in his sentry box. Bostonian anger at the unwelcome presence of British soldiers had reached a riot pitch. A mob pelted the sentry and eight other soldiers who had gone to his aid. The fracas, which left five rioters dead, can hardly be classed as a massacre, and the mob was clearly at fault. No matter how we memorialize it, that is where it actually happened.

Another oddity on the Freedom Trail can be found at the Old North Church. Some controversy still exists as to whether this was really the steeple from which lanterns flashed news that the British were moving toward Lexington, but apparently no controversy exists about the fact that from this same steeple, a man once flew—in 1757! A plaque mounted on the brick wall of the churchyard reads:

Here on September 13, 1757, John Childs who had given public notice of his intention to fly from the steeple of Dr.

Cutler's church performed it to the satisfaction of a great number of spectators.

What the plaque does not say is that the very next day, he did it again. And not just once, but twice.

According to the Boston *News Letter* for the week of September 8–15, 1757, on the final trip of the second day, "he set off with two pistols loaded, one of which he discharged in his descent; the other missing fire, he cocked and snapped again before he reached the Place prepared to receive him." We don't know exactly where Childs came to earth, but the *News Letter* said it was on a slope about seven hundred feet away from the steeple. Each flight was estimated to have taken sixteen to eighteen seconds.

Surprisingly, the newspaper account failed to describe *how* Childs managed to fly through the air. However he did it, John Childs' flights were a local sensation. Having satisfied an expectant crowd the first day, he drew even a larger one for his next flight. Unfortunately, the two days were a Tuesday and a Wednesday, days on which serious men should be about their business and not loitering in streets to be amused by frivolous spectacles performed from church steeples. With a frown, Boston's town fathers clipped Childs' airborne antics by proclaiming that "he is forbid flying any more in the Town."

Boston has another oddity that should not be missed. Fifteen feet above the sidewalk on Court Street, the largest tea kettle in America gleams like gold overhead. (It used to hang lower, but trucks kept banging into it, and one time that happened, some thief also swiped the lid.) There's no symbolic connection between the giant kettle and Boston's famous Tea Party. Rigged to have steam always rising from its spout, it was created as an advertisement for the Oriental Tea Company and may be America's oldest advertising sign. Hung in 1873, it has been kept steaming through fair weather and foul—and that's a long time to keep the pot a'boiling.

At the time it went on display, its capacity was unknown. Coppersmiths had made it entirely "by eye"; they took no measure-

America's largest tea kettle

ments because they never expected to make another one. Almost immediately, questions were raised about how much the kettle would hold, so the owners decided to measure it in a public ceremony. On New Year's Day in 1875, a crowd of more than ten thousand persons gathered to watch the city sealer of weights and measures perform his official duty.

Just before the process of measuring began, the kettle's lid was removed, and out climbed a twelve-year-old boy. He was followed by another—and another—and another—until finally eight boys stood in front of the kettle, bowing to the applauding crowd. As they took their bows, a six-foot man wearing a polished beaver hat climbed out of the kettle behind them. The kettle's capacity was then measured at a bit more than 227 gallons.

Should you happen to head into South Boston across the Congress Street Bridge, you won't be able to ignore the giant milk bottle. A vintage lunch stand from the 1930s era, the thirty-foot-tall Hood Milk bottle still serves snacks today.

Cambridge is across the river from Boston but the two towns are linked by history as well as a number of bridges. Standing near a giant elm on Cambridge Common, George Washington took formal command of the Continental Army in 1775. At 175 Brattle Street stands the Ruggles Fayerweather House, first owned by Tory George Ruggles and later by patriot Thomas Fayerweather. It was used as an American hospital after the Battle of Bunker Hill.

Army hospitals then were local buildings pressed into emergency service. Washington had to create an army hospital system. He chose Dr. Benjamin Church, an ardent patriot, as America's first surgeon general. Dr. Church turned the Ruggles Fayerweather house into the first hospital of the American army and ran it with considerable ability and good sense. When Church later asked to be relieved of his duties, Washington declined on the grounds that he was reluctant "to part with a good officer." A week later Dr. Church was under arrest as a British spy.

Seems the good doctor had been in constant and secret communication with British general Gage. When Gage sent British troops to Lexington and Concord, he was acting on information Church had supplied about arms being stored there. A full month before the Bunker Hill battle, Church forwarded to Gage news about the colonial plans for fortifying the hill. (Fortunately, Gage failed to act on Church's information.) Church was tripped up when one of his secret messages got sidetracked and was eventually deciphered by Americans. He was exiled to the West Indies under threat of death if he ever returned. Whether or not he got there is unknown, since the schooner carrying him was never heard from again.

Anyone who visits Cambridge will be tempted to stroll through Harvard Yard. It's a walk through history—with an occasional misstep. Along a diagonal path across Old Yard is the Daniel French statue of John Harvard. The dedication of this famous statue does contain a few errors. It has the wrong date for the founding of Harvard, it doesn't depict John Harvard (since the sculptor didn't know what Harvard looked like, he used a student as his model), and John Harvard did not found Harvard College (though he was its first great benefactor). French's sculpture is known locally as "the statue of the three lies."

England had its Tudor kings and New England had one too. Frederic Tudor became New England's "Ice King." Much of his wealth and fame came from Cambridge's Fresh Pond and the nearby Walden Pond. There was nothing new about farmers using ice to keep produce from spoiling, but it seems Tudor invented the ice business. His first effort was a shipload of ice to Martinique in 1806. The proprietor of the Tivoli Gardens, who had never seen ice, reluctantly allowed Tudor to freeze "ice creams" to be sold over the counter. They brought in more than three hundred dollars on the first night. Hunting for an effective insulation against heat, Tudor tried packing ice in rice chaff, wheat, tan bark, coal dust, and pulverized cork. The ice still melted. Then he tried pine dust and knew it was the answer.

To improve his production of ice, Tudor hired Nathaniel Wyatt, who devised special saws and tools to bore through the ice, cut it into blocks, and move it along a beltway to a warehouse. Now needing new markets, Tudor invaded India. One of his cargoes arrived at Calcutta, having been at sea in tropical waters for four months with little loss from melting. In 1849, Tudor shipped 150,000 tons of ice to Persia, the East and West Indies, South America, and San Francisco. By 1864 he was shipping ice to fifty-three ports around the world. He had truly become the Ice King.

Lynn is northeast of Boston along U.S. 1. In one corner is Lynn Woods, a two thousand–acre park located next to the Saugus-Lynn border. Within its wild, natural beauty are many oddities, available to those strolling along the walking trails. Walden Pond is not Thoreau's but the less celebrated one named for Edwin Walden, mayor of Lynn. Great Frog Boulder bears an uneasy resemblance to an open-mouthed frog ready to snap at a fly. The stone-lined, rectangular Wolf Pits were used to trap wolves. As late as 1735, hunters gathered there to kill the predators. Nearby is Lantern

Rock, where pirates once hung signal lights for small boats stealing up the Saugus River at night.

Of all the pirate treasure tales along the Atlantic coast, the one about Pirates' Glen and Dungeon Rock is probably the strangest. On a pleasant evening in the 1650s, a strange vessel anchored near the mouth of the Saugus River. Four men rowed ashore and disappeared into the woods. The vessel was gone by the next morning but a paper had been left behind, requesting that iron handcuffs, shackles, hatchets, and other items from the local iron works be secretly deposited at a certain location, and promising full payment in silver at the same spot when the goods were picked up. The exchange was made, and months later the glen became a haven for the four pirates. Before long, however, a king's cruiser hunted them down and three of the pirates were captured in their glen. The fourth, Thomas Veal, escaped and took refuge inside a spacious cavern within a large rock. This is now called Dungeon Rock. Veal lived there as a practicing shoemaker, although many believed him to be guardian of treasure buried in the cave by the pirates. Then in 1658, a great earthquake shook the area. The top of Veal's rock was loosened and crashed down into the mouth of his cavern, imprisoning him forever. Part of the opening is still visible today.

The quake failed to shake local belief that pirates had buried some treasure in the cavern. Treasure hunters brought down more of the cavern roof with a keg of gunpowder in 1834. Hiram Marble purchased the site in 1852 and under spiritual direction from mediums and clairvoyants, began to tunnel through the solid rock. With his son Edwin, he drilled holes deep into the rock, poured blasting powder into them, lit fuses, and scurried out of the cave. The debris was hauled out and new holes were drilled. By 1863 they had dug a hole through solid rock that was about 135 feet long and about 7 feet high and 7 feet wide. Hiram Marble died in 1868; Edwin died in 1880. Their efforts uncovered no pirate treasure, but they were convinced they had discovered the sword of Thomas Veal or one of his companions at the farthest extremity of their excavation. (They refused to believe later admissions from people who had deliberately planted the sword where it would be found.)

Farther up the coast along Route 127 is Magnolia. The treacherous Norman's Woe Rock is just off the coast behind the Hammond Castle Museum, and your best view of it is from there. The rock probably inspired Longfellow to write "The Wreck of the Hesperus," in which the stricken vessel is swept "Tow'rds the reef of Norman's Woe." (The Hammond Castle Museum is on Hesperus Avenue, which turns into Norman Avenue; no one knows who Norman was or why he was woeful.) The Hammond Castle Museum is an oddity in itself. John Hammond designed the castle as a setting for his art collections. He was fascinated by the bizarre and the Gothic. His creation has a Roman bath, secret passages, peepholes, and a colossal organ. Hammond designed the ten thousand organ pipes himself. The inner courtyard has its own weather system that can produce a tropical downpour and follow it up with sunshine. And in the courtyard patio, turned modestly seaward, is a nude statue of himself.

Located on Hesperus Avenue about halfway between the castle and the center of Magnolia is a small parking lot surrounded by woods and a chain-link fence. A short walk through the woods leads to the red granite shore and Rafe's Chasm, a fissure sixty feet deep and six to ten feet wide. For two hundred feet it cuts back into a rocky ledge—it's over to the far left as you face the water. Leif Eriksson's brother Thorwald was killed there by Indians back in A.D. 1004, and others have died since by being careless on the rocks. (If it's not pirates, it's Vikings!)

Route 127 will also take you up to Rockport on Cape Ann, a town crowded by tourists anxious to capture on film their own version of a special lobster shack on the water's edge. It's a red building that has been depicted by artists so often that it is affectionately known as "Motif No. 1." The original shack that attracted them is long gone—destroyed in a blizzard in 1978. However, its charm was so popular that funds were raised to rebuild it. The oddity is that while many people today believe "Motif No. 1" is a genuine Cape Ann antique, it is really just an authentic reproduction.

At 52 Pigeon Hill Street in the Pigeon Cove section of Rockport, you can see a unique house built by the Stenman family. It took twenty years to finish. It began as an experiment in 1922 to see what could be done architecturally with newspapers. Except for the

roof, floors, doors, windows, and fireplace, the house was made entirely out of newspapers—rolled or folded, then glued and var-
nished! More than 100,000 daily editions were used. The walls are
215 pages thick. Look carefully at the window decorations and
beaded strings. Even the furniture is made of newspaper. On part of
the writing desk, one can still read an account of Lindbergh's historic flight. A grandfather clock is made of newspapers from the
capital cities of what was then only forty-eight states. Magazine
sections from the Sunday Boston *Herald* and the New York *Herald
Tribune* make up the massive, ceiling-high mantel over the fireplace. A cot is constructed of papers saved since World War I. The
newspaper piano still plays!

Incidentally, it was at Rockport in 1710 that an ingenious Yankee named Joshua Norwood began using granite as a mooring
stone. After drilling a hole in the center of a stone, he would jam an
oak tree down through it, roots and all. While roots and stone
rested firmly on the bottom of shallow water in the bay, his boat
would be securely tied to the top of the tree above the surface.
(Now that's recycling!)

You have to travel a bit along Routes 127, 128, 133, and 1-A to
go from Rockport to Newburyport, but that's where Timothy Dexter spent most of his life and where he is buried. Dexter was an il-
literate, preposterous, and gullible buffoon, the constant target of
public ridicule. He was also a financial enigma. Only twenty-three
when he married a wealthy widow in 1770, he used her money to
support his impossible ventures—which were invariably successful.
During and after the Revolutionary War, Dexter bought up all of
the worthless state bonds no one else wanted. After Alexander
Hamilton carried out his financial reforms, Dexter's bonds were re-
deemed in full. Envious merchants detested his success. When they
maliciously suggested he buy warming pans to sell in the West Indies, he did—and made another fortune; the tops were used as
strainers and the bottoms became long-handled ladles for use in
making molasses. Thinking they were pulling his leg, other hoax-
ters urged Dexter to send Bibles and mittens to heathens in the
tropics. Both sold well; ships heading toward Arctic waters from
the tropics bought all of the mittens and the Bibles arrived just as a

missionary drive for Christianity got under way. He followed local advice to ship coal to the coal-mining town of Newcastle in England and made a bundle because his cargoes arrived during a miners' strike. When a ship's carpenter derisively suggested he invest in "wales" (by which he meant heavy planks fastened to the outside of hulls on wooden ships), Dexter cornered the market on whalebones, which had no value at all until women began wearing corsets shaped with them! In Dexter's day, Newburyport was overrun with stray cats of all sizes and shapes; every effort to get rid of the cats failed. Dexter advertised that during a ten-day period, he would pay a small sum of two or three pennies for every caged cat delivered to his wharf. At the end of the ten days, he pointed to an island on the map that his captains had never visited and told them to try selling the cats there. The island happened to be covered with plantations, and they, in turn, were covered with mice and rats. The islanders fought to buy the cats and Dexter sold all two thousand of them, some for as high as five or six dollars each, a small fortune in the eighteenth century. Timothy Dexter and his wife are buried somewhere in Newburyport's Old Burying Ground.

However, Mary Mchard is buried in Old Hill Cemetery. According to the epitaph, at her death on March 8, 1780, "the throbbing hearts of her disconsolate family confessed their fairest prospects of sublunary bless were, in one moment dashed" when Mary Mchard swallowed a pea. There are no details about how it caused her death a few hours later. ("Sublunary" means "under the moon.") If it's true that there's nothing new under the sun, it might also be true that (to quote the poet John Dryden) "all things sublunary are subject to change." This change was caused by a pea.

Haverhill is west of Newburyport. Capt. Nathaniel Thurston's grave in the Old Bradford Cemetery heads a line of seven tombstones. Six mark the burial sites of wives he married between 1790 and 1806. Sometimes he buried two wives within one year. The gravestones indicate that he had no trouble attracting the attention of women much younger than himself. Reportedly, one of the later brides said he was so attractive, she just couldn't refuse to marry him. His last bride outlived him and is not buried there. Along with the undertaker, she accompanied his coffin from a New York town to the Haverhill cemetery. Upon the completion of the return journey, she married the undertaker.

Heading southwest on I-495, you can easily find the Lowell National Historical Park by following signs into the center of Lowell from the highway. The park's history contains an oddity that is seldom mentioned. Francis Cabot Lowell was the originator of the American cotton manufacturing industry. Through his early efforts, the textile industry was born in Lowell and the town became the industrial marvel of the world.

The little-known oddity lies in how all of this came about. In the early years of the nineteenth century, the British held a monopoly on the manufacture of cloth because they had developed a power loom to replace the time-consuming use of hand looms. Naturally, plans for building a power loom were carefully guarded. By law, sending plans or drawings out of the country was strictly prohibited, and anyone knowledgeable about the workings of a power loom was forced to remain in England.

Francis Lowell was not an industrialist but a shrewd merchant and trader, so well connected that British friends escorted him through their textile factories, unaware that he was planning to move into industrial competition. Somehow Lowell memorized the important details about power looms. He was an adept mathematician who observed details carefully and remembered them. He would not have been allowed to carry drawings or sketches out of the country, and indeed, he and his luggage were searched thoroughly before he left England. When he got back to America, he contacted his friend Paul Moody, a superb mechanic. Between what Lowell had memorized and what Moody deduced from it, they put together a power loom superior to the British original. The British textile monopoly was broken.

South of Lowell, Route 38 passes through Wilmington, where the most elaborate funeral in New England took place on May 23, 1900. Drs. Henry and Frances Hiller moved to Wilmington from Boston. Both were interested in the hereafter and agreed to spend their money on the creation of two elaborate, ornate caskets. They hired a woodcarver and cabinetmaker named James MacGregor, who told them that even with his four assistants it would take him seven years to do the carvings they requested. Henry died before his casket was finished, and so burial was delayed a year. Hers was finished three and a half years later. Frances was so pleased, she displayed it in her parlor, reclining within it to demonstrate to her friends how she would look.

The inner shell and outer casket together weighed over a ton and cost nearly thirty thousand dollars, a king's ransom in those days. The outside had ivy vines, a skull with a lizard crawling out of one eye, angels, cupids, and dragons by the dozen. A perching owl held a tiny mouse in its claws. The cover of the inner box had gold and silver plates engraved with portraits of the couple and their many children. Her twenty thousand–dollar burial robe was made of corded silk, trimmed with five hundred yards of handmade silk lace, and hand embroidered with over five thousand daisies. The mausoleum was to be forty feet square and forty feet high with plate glass windows behind bronze gratings. (In reality it became a ten-foot-high tomb at the entrance to Wildwood Cemetery.) Frances Hiller's funeral car was too high to pass under trolley wires, so carpenters hastily reduced its height by fourteen inches to nineteen feet. Thousands of curious mourners clogged the streets during the procession, and like year-round residents when summer visitors have gone, Wilmington breathed a sigh of relief as the tomb door closed. However, the tomb soon became an eyesore. It was demolished in 1935 and the two caskets buried where the tomb had been. They are still there, marked only by two large stone urns above two simple bronze plaques. Her first name was misspelled as "France."

If you'd like to see something really far out, head southward to Wellesley Hills just west of where Route 9 crosses I-95. There, at Babson College, the world's largest revolving globe, twenty-eight feet in diameter, weighing twenty-five tons that rotate on a six-ton axis, depicts Earth as it would appear from five thousand miles out in space. It can simulate day and night as well as seasonal changes. The nearby Map and Globe Museum contains the world's largest relief map of the United States. It is sixty-five feet long and forty-five feet wide with a curved surface that is topographically accurate. It took fifteen years to build. You can see what the United States looks like from seven hundred miles away.

Still farther south on I-95 is Sharon, where Deborah Sampson lived part of her life. The house she lived in is just off of East Street near a pond. She is buried in Sharon's Rock Ridge Cemetery but a statue in her honor stands in front of the public library. A street in Sharon is named after her. Two names appear on her gravestone. Both belonged to her. Under the assumed name Robert Shurtleff, Deborah Sampson became the first female soldier in the Continental Army during the Revolutionary War!

One of seven children in a fatherless household, Deborah was indentured to a comfortable farm family in which there were ten sons. She preferred working in the fields with them to doing household chores. Five feet seven and a half inches tall (at a time when men averaged five feet four and women only four feet nine), Deborah acquired her adopted brothers' masculine mannerisms and customs. Stirred by hearing the Declaration of Independence read aloud, Deborah passed herself off as a man and enlisted in the Fourth Massachusetts Regiment under the name of "Robert Shurtleff." Her rigorous farm chores had given her the strength to carry her firearm, bayonet, hatchet, cartridge box, buckshot and leaden balls, flint and powder, jackknife, canteen, haversack, and blanket.

Legend has it that Deborah was at Yorktown when Cornwallis surrendered. That is not true, but she did take part in several military battles and was wounded during one at Tarrytown, suffering a saber slash in the head and at least one bullet, perhaps two, in her thigh. Desperate to avoid medical examination that would reveal she was a woman, Deborah focused the surgeon's attention on her head wound and secretly extracted the bullet or bullets in her thigh by herself. It wasn't until several months later, during action at Philadelphia, that Deborah's secret was discovered when she came down with typhoid fever. While she was unconscious, a startled doctor unveiled her bound breasts. He kept her secret while she recovered but insisted that Gen. Washington be told. She received an honorable discharge in 1783 but without the usual soldier's pension. Paul Revere aided her in securing a small pension and some back pay.

After Deborah's death in 1827, her husband applied for a widower's pension—the first ever! In granting his request, Congress finally recognized Deborah Sampson as a fully accredited soldier and war hero. The Commonwealth of Massachusetts had already done so in 1792. Awarding her compensation for military service, the old record includes: "And, whereas, it further appears that the said Deborah exhibited an extraordinary instance of female heroism by discharging the duties of a faithful, gallant soldier, and at the same time preserved the virtue and chastity of her sex unsuspected and unblemished, & was discharged from the service with a fair & honorable character."

Upton is west of Sharon—about twenty-two miles as the crow flies. It's longer along the several local roads one must use to get there. Since the oddity in Upton is on private property, and permission must be obtained before viewing, you might want to skip Upton. If you do, you will have passed up the chance to see an unusual architectural puzzle. A few yards off of Elm Street is an ancient man-made stone cave. It remains today as it was when first discovered—a large, circular chamber with a domed roof connected to a long, narrow entranceway. It's about twenty-four feet from the entrance to the rear of the chamber, which is about eleven feet in diameter and ten feet high. Slabs of stone weighing many tons had to be moved into place using sophisticated engineering techniques. A 1980 study concluded that the architectural scheme used to interface the passageway to the domed chamber is "the only stone chamber known to exhibit this specific architectural feature in the United States. The only other known intact chambers that present this feature are located in Ireland—the passage, roofed with lintel slabs, rises as it approaches the circular chamber, which has soaring, corbelled roof. . . ." They concluded that the Upton chamber had been built around the year 710. By whom or how? No answers yet.

If you've skipped Upton, perhaps you've gone on to Worcester. One oddity there is in the north part of the city, where the geographic center of Massachusetts is located.

Leominster is north of Worcester on I-190. Many people have heard that Johnny Appleseed was born there, but in spite of much publicity in various forms, few people know anything at all about the persecution of Joseph Palmer, who is buried there. He wasn't persecuted in Leominster—that took place around Fitchburg, which is down the road.

From Chinese pigtails to powdered wigs and sideburns, we seem to pay much more attention to what is on the outside of our head than what is within it. The temporary martyrdom of Joseph Palmer came about simply because he wore a beard! Well, maybe it wasn't just that. He was a temperance man who refused to serve rum to the men working his fields. When they boycotted him, he hired boys to replace the strikers. That irked one irate mother, who refused to let her son work for "a man so mean that he won't give the boys a drop of liquor." But when Joseph Palmer began growing his beard, he became the target of public wrath.

In Joseph Palmer's day, a beard was positively sinful. However, Palmer was a religious man who once defended his beard to his preacher by telling him that Satan was always depicted as clean-shaven while Christ wore a beard. He was also a thoughtful man who believed that nature intended man to wear hair on his face— that's why it grows there. In reply to one person who asked why he wore a beard, Palmer wondered aloud why anyone should waste the time taken up by shaving every day.

One day Palmer was set upon by four men armed with shears and razors, determined to remove his beard. Thrown to the ground and injured, Palmer swiped at their legs with an old jackknife. They turned him in for unprovoked assault and the judge found him guilty of "disturbing the peace by wearing a beard." As a matter of principle, Palmer refused to pay the twenty-dollar fine. Jailed, he successfully and physically defended himself against a regulation that prisoners be shaved once a week. Letters he smuggled out to his son about being jailed for wearing a beard began appearing in local papers and public apathy turned into public sympathy. Officials urged him to leave the jail but Palmer said he had been illegally incarcerated and would stay there until his right to wear a beard was publicly affirmed. In 1831 he was bodily carried out of the jail after more than a year behind bars—and the jail door hastily locked behind him!

While Palmer was still alive, soldiers in the Revolutionary War were always clean-shaven; their counterparts during the Civil War became bearded. When Lincoln was elected, he had no beard but grew one in time for his inauguration. As a lieutenant, Grant wore an unnoticeable mustache; as a general he wore a full beard. During the Civil War, beards became a badge of solid worth and a symbol of great integrity. In the Evergreen Cemetery in North Leominster, stands a tall white monument in honor of Joseph Palmer that shows Palmer's head with its magnificent beard and bears the caption, "Persecuted for Wearing the Beard."

North of Leominster on Route 13 is Townsend. Along the north side of Route 119 in Townsend is what looks like a school building—exactly what it was built to be. The Spaulding School has a weather vane on top that looks like an owl. Take a closer look. It's really a bat. A bat as a weather vane for a school? According to current theory, a wise old owl was supposed to be the weather vane but probably was not forged in time for the dedication ceremony. An available bat was a last minute substitute in the hope that no one would know the difference. Apparently few people did.

Gardner is astride Route 2 west of Leominster. Of the approximately twenty octagonal houses in Massachusetts, one is at the corner of Green and Heywood streets. A better oddity exists nearby. In front of the school at 130 Elm Street is New England's tallest chair. Gardner bills itself as the "Chair City of the World" because the manufacture of chairs was its major industry. Honoring that title in 1976, the Rotary Club commissioned Leon W. LaPlante to design and build the giant chair, which he completed after eight weeks of labor. The chair is over twenty feet high. (Unfortunately for Gardner, the largest chair in the United States was built for a furniture store in Binghamton, New York. It is twenty-four feet, nine inches high.)

What is believed to be the world's largest rocking horse can be seen in Winchendon, northwest of Gardner along Routes 140 and 12. It is an exact replica of the first such horse given to the town in 1914. For many years this one stood on the grounds of Converse Toy Manufacturers. The plant burned down and the horse deteriorated so badly that it had to be restored. This new hand-carved gi-

World's largest rocking horse

ant is ten feet tall and weighs a ton and a half. It can be seen in front of the VFW building at the intersection of Routes 12 and 202.

Another interesting sign, or pair of signs, can be seen south of Winchendon along U.S. 202 just outside of Baldwinville. Side by side are two highway markers. One says you are on Route 202 north and the other says you are on Route 68 south. Of course, if you are going in the opposite direction it would be 202 south and 68 north. Go figure.

If you head over toward Athol and turn south on Route 32, you'll come into Petersham. Just beyond the far end of the town common (at the intersection of Routes 32 and 122) is a house that demonstrates how far New Englanders can go to express their opinions. Unlike most houses, this one doesn't face either of the two roads that pass it. In fact, the house has its back turned on the town. An early and ingenious owner named Forester Goddard had many talents and was an excellent stonemason who took great pride in his work. In 1886 he was hired by the town to repair and rebuild the west wall of the village cemetery. No doubt he did a good job; the wall appears as sturdy today as when it was built. But building it cost more than the town had agreed to pay. Unable to collect what he thought was right, Goddard decided to express his opinion about the town. With no one to help him except his wife, Goddard began to slowly and carefully jack up their house, which measured twenty-seven feet by ten feet. Then he placed leveling planks under it. Using croquet balls as ball bearings, he lowered his house until it rested on the croquet balls. Slowly he inched the house around until its backside faced the town he now despised. The house is in that same position today.

If you go south on U.S. 202 from the Athol area, you'll come to Pelham. (History books mention Shays' Rebellion. Pelham is where Capt. Daniel Shays led eight hundred angry farmers in an unsuccessful tax revolt.) The town hall is the real oddity in Pelham. Built in 1743, it is the oldest town hall in New England to have been in continuous use. Pelham citizens must also have been among New England's hardiest. Records show that the building remained unheated until 1831. The town hall is inconveniently located, but Pelham maintains its record by holding at least one town meeting there annually.

The building next to the town hall was originally the Congregational Church but is now the historical society's museum. Locked within is the "genuine duplicate" Poison Oyster Stone that marked the burial site of one Warren Gibbs in the Knights Cemetery just west of U.S. 202 on Packardville Road. The epitaph is an open accusation that Warren's wife killed him by putting arsenic in his oysters. Her family was furious. The stone was stolen, recovered, and finally disappeared, probably destroyed. The duplicate stone that replaced it was stolen in 1940. What happened to the duplicate? Seven years later it was discovered buried in a dirt basement. It can be seen in the museum of the Pelham Historical Society, which prudently erected yet another stone copy over Warren Gibbs's grave.

The famed Mohawk Trail starts at Greenfield, northwest of Pelham. If you take this scenic route west, you'll enjoy great vistas and encounter some hairpin turns. At North Adams you will come across the only natural marble bridge in North America. (It's a half mile northeast of the town on Route 8. Look for signs to the Natural Bridge State Park.) Formed by water erosion, the bridge spans a chasm 60 feet deep that winds through 475 feet of rock more than 550 million years old. Seashells deposited here by the ocean were piled so high that their own weight compressed them into limestone. Then the Berkshire Mountains began to build, buckle, and fold. Limestone was metamorphosed and recrystallized into marble by the tremendous pressure and heat created during mountain formation.

Following Route 8 south from there would bring you into Cheshire—and the only monument in the world dedicated to a really big cheese. Back in 1801, Baptist minister John Leland persuaded local farmers to contribute one day's milk toward making a colossal cheese for President Thomas Jefferson. On the appointed day, farmers came from miles around with donations collected from nine hundred cows. No cheese press was large enough to handle all of the curds, so they used a reinforced cider press, but even that wasn't enough. The main cheese wheel was as big as a bass drum and weighed 1,450 pounds, while three smaller cheeses weighed 70 pounds each. The giant cheese was pressed for a whole month, then carefully removed from the press and ripened for many weeks in a cheese house. It had to be turned over daily without cracking it. After being safely transported by land and water, it arrived at the White House in a cart drawn by six horses and bearing a sign: THE GREATEST CHEESE IN AMERICA FOR THE GREATEST MAN IN AMERICA. When presented to him on New Year's Day 1802 in the East Room of the White House, President Jefferson quipped that the cows must have all been Republicans and gave Leland two hundred dollars rather than accept a gift from poor farmers. As he cut the first slice, the president said, "I will cause this auspicious event to be placed on the records of our nation and it will ever shine amid its glorious archives." The cheese continued to be served at the White House for the next three years. The monument in Chester is a replica of the cider press and displays a tablet honoring Leland, Jefferson, and the cheese itself.

Where Route 8 runs into Route 9 south of Chester is Coltsville —and the Allendale Shopping Center. Upended as the centerpiece

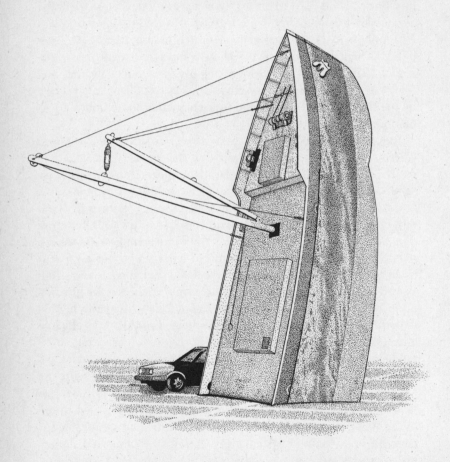

The Sea Bee

of its parking area is the thirty-two-foot bow of the *Sea Bee*, a vessel used for many years to service and fuel fishing vessels working out of Boston Harbor. Built in 1948, the *Sea Bee* had finally been left sitting in saltwater and sinking twice a day at high tide. Sculptor Dustin Shuler arranged to have the fifteen-ton bow severed from the rest of the ship, rebuilt the bow's mast and rigging, and painted the bottom red, the hull black, the trim white, and the anchors silver. The bow is pointed skyward and planted firmly in a concrete block. Shuler says his concept is not political but simply art. Most observers would agree. Is the ship sinking, stern first? Or is it rising hopefully out of a troubled sea? The *Sea Bee* may seem inappropriate in a Berkshire shopping mall, but like a mustache on the *Mona Lisa*, it makes you stop and think. There are other artistic goodies scattered around the mall. On the walkway in front are temple bells, a device containing the pleasing sound of rushing water, and an abstract display of moving lights. Near the outer edge of the area is a large model of a sailplane, gently doing spins and barrel rolls atop a slender spindle. The underground section of the mall contains similar creations on its walls.

In 1903 two lionesses escaped from a circus cage in nearby Pittsfield. Ferocious enough to mangle two draft horses tethered nearby, one was cornered and had to be killed. The other fled down nearby streets and eventually encountered Mrs. Patrick McCarty, returning from a grocery shop. The lioness swung an enormous paw at Mrs. McCarty's bag of fresh meat. Outraged, Mrs. McCarty swung her umbrella and clouted the lioness between the eyes. The vicious lioness yelped and fled. Cowed by the encounter, she later surrendered peacefully.

Tyringham is not on a major route but is worth finding. (On a map, look south of the small town of Lee and near Exit 2 on I-90.) It has been said that Tyringham is so sleepy on a summer day that the dogs ignore the cats. What you won't be able to ignore on the main road through town is the Tyringham Art Gallery. The structure is one of the most outstanding examples of personal architecture in New England. Designed as a sculpture studio by the late Sir Henry Kitson, it was built in the early 1930s, with the reconstructed rear portions dating back about 150 years. Kitson called his estate "Santarella" and, for privacy, had it completely hidden from the road by a heavy brush fence. (Kitson sculpted the minuteman statue at Lexington. The Englishman he used for his model later became a U.S. citizen, a national heavyweight wrestling champion, and a national canoe-paddling champion.)

Small studios on the upper level of Kitson's structure had trap doors through which heavy sculpture could be lowered to the main floor. The roof was made of conventional materials, cut to look like thatching and shaped to resemble the rolling hills of the Berkshires. It is actually a giant sculpture made of shingles over a period of two years by English workers imported for that purpose. The roof weighs eighty tons and is supported by a massive armature of heavy chestnut beams. Tremendous rocks were brought in by horse and stone boat. Grottoes were created between the rock pillars to emulate similar features in Europe. The wild gardens in the rear attracted birds. The pond once held goldfish that Kitson fed with oatmeal.

Finally, Quabbin Reservoir is the world's largest man-made do-

Tyringham Art Gallery

mestic water supply impoundment. Created in central Massachusetts by damming the Swift River, the reservoir supplies water to the Boston area. Capable of holding more than four hundred billion gallons, it lives up to its Indian name "Quabbin," which means "a lot of water." More than fifty islands were created when the valley was flooded, and four towns were submerged.

RHODE ISLAND

Rhode Island has many odd qualities. First, it's not an island at all. The smallest state in our nation, it has the longest name: officially it is The State of Rhode Island and Providence Plantations. A continuous controversy between the Dutch and the English centered around place names, since the language of regional names was frequently cited as proof of discovery. A Dutchman in 1630 had used the term *Roode Eyland* (meaning little reddish island), so in 1644 the Court of Providence Plantation circumvented the Dutch name by declaring "that the island commonly called Aquethneck, shall be from henceforth called the Isle of Rhodes, or Rhode Island." The Massachusetts General Court, disdaining the new name as presumptuous, usually spelled it Road Island.

Bordering Rhode Island's 1,214 square miles are some four hundred miles of coastline and more than one hundred public beaches. Though more densely populated than any other state except New Jersey, Rhode Island has about eighteen thousand acres of park land and more than 20 percent of all of the registered historic landmarks in the entire country. It's also the only state in New England that doesn't have a covered bridge. Once there were five. All disappeared by 1920 except one, the Hamlet Bridge, a railroad bridge in the industrial heart of Woonsocket. Lop-eared in appearance because it had to be built at an angle, the Hamlet Bridge was destroyed by Hurricane Diane in August 1955—and then there were none.

Rhode Islanders claim that no place in the state is more than a forty-five-minute drive from anywhere else. They've forgotten about Block Island, which is an additional one-hour ferry ride from Point Judith. The Indians living there called it Manisses ("Manitou's Little Island"). The first European to explore the island, Adriaen Block, had previously discovered the Connecticut River. Block named the small island Adriaen's Eylant, but custom soon created its current name. Today visitors are welcome, but in the past, some intruders got short shrift. On the chalky cliffs at Mohegan Bluffs, the local tribe of Narragansett Indians pushed a band of Mohegan invaders over the bluffs onto the rocks two hundred feet below. Not every arrival met such a fate. At Settlers' Rock on the shore of Cow Cove is a huge field stone with a bronze tablet listing the names of Block Island's first settlers, who landed there in April 1661. The cove is named for the first cow on the island (known locally as the "cow settler"), which probably swam ashore from a shipwreck.

Shipwrecks—and legends about them—plague Block Islanders. The most popular centers on a doomed ship from Rotterdam (unnamed but called *Palatine*) that ran aground on Sandy Point sometime around 1720. Apparently abandoned by its crew, the passengers were either dead or at the point of starvation. Block Islanders rescued sixteen survivors, but one passenger refused to abandon her possessions on the ship. A storm came up, driving the burning ship off the reef, and the last passenger's screams were heard as it drifted out to sea. For many years thereafter, mysterious lights appeared in the area—curious illuminations, said by some to resemble the image of a blazing ship, rising up from the waters and then disappearing beneath the waves. These are known as the *Palatine* lights. The *Palatine* survivors are buried in Palatine Cemetery.

Block Islanders are attentive to their environment. The Southeast Lighthouse at Mohegan Bluffs was recently moved two hundred feet inland from the eroding bluffs. A sign at an ancient glacial crevice called Rodman's Hollow asks that visitors respect the land "so that all human, creature and plant life may share in its peace and beauty." Along the northern shore of Block Island's Great Salt Pond is Beane Point, where many endangered species are being preserved. Oddly enough, this environmental haven was brought about by the discovery that marijuana had been grown there. The land was seized by the police, as required by law. After nearly four years of negotiations with the other two co-owners of the property, twenty-three acres on Beane Point became an ecological safety zone for a wide variety of migrating birds.

The mainland of Rhode Island is so fragmented by the state's many lakes, ponds, rivers, and bays that it is rarely possible to outline a simple route from any one location to another. For example, probably the nation's oldest carousel is in Watch Hill, down in the extreme southwest corner of Rhode Island and not on any heavily traveled tourist route, in spite of its lovely beaches and ocean vistas. The Flying Horse Carousel at Watch Hill was built in 1870 and was in use before 1879. Its precise origin remains a mystery. According to local legend, a traveling circus run by gypsies came to town one day in late summer more than a hundred years ago. Virtually penniless when they arrived, the gypsies later abandoned the carousel and vanished. It survived burial under tons of sand kicked up by a 1938 hurricane. Whether or not this carousel predates the other Flying Horse Carousel on Martha's Vineyard (see page 90) may be a moot point, since the latter's horses move up and down on vertical poles while the Watch Hill horses, suspended by chains from a central hub, swing outward as the hub rotates—they really seem to fly! Each horse has been hand carved from a single piece of wood with agate eyes and leather saddles. The tails and manes are real horsehair. Small riders still grab for brass rings, storing the less valuable ones on the pointed ears of their horse for safekeeping. Children whose feet can touch the floor after they swing into the saddle are deemed too old to ride.

Northeast of Watch Hill, U.S. 1 and Route 2 lead to the Great Swamp, where Metacomet, the Indian leader known to white men as King Philip, suffered his greatest defeat in King Philip's War

(1675–76). King Philip was chief of the Wampanoag Indians, who found themselves caught between the colonies of Plymouth and Connecticut, both of which were competing for Indian land. As King Philip pointed out in 1674, whenever disputes arose between whites and Indians, it was always settled in the white man's court and the Indians were forced to pay in land for all damages assessed. Angered by the continual harassment and humiliation, King Philip negotiated an alliance with the Narragansett and Nipmuck Indians, and King Philip's War began. On December 18, 1675, a colonial army of one thousand men attacked the Narragansett Indian stronghold in the frozen swamp. Although some Indians escaped, six hundred men, women, and children were killed during the fight and an unknown number perished when the colonials set fire to the Indian wigwams. The Great Swamp fight hardened Indian resolve and King Philip's War spread out into Connecticut and Massachusetts, ending only with King Philip's death in 1676. Today the Great Swamp is a twenty-six-hundred-acre wildlife refuge with a granite shaft marking the site of the Indian fort.

Crompton is one mile north-northeast of Rhode Island's geographic center. Almost directly east of Crompton and on the edge of Narragansett Bay is Warwick. In a cemetery on West Shore Road, John Wickes is buried in two separate side-by-side graves. Fearing an Indian attack during King Philip's War, most settlers abandoned their homes and left the area in 1675. A few elected to stay behind in Thomas Greene's garrison house, built of solid stone and thought to be impervious to attack. Wickes was among those who remained to watch helplessly from its safety one day as King Philip's warriors appeared, burned the rest of the township, and drove the livestock off into the woods. After they had gone, Wickes decided to leave the garrison house and search for his scattered cattle. As a longtime friend of the Indians, he thought he would be safe—but he was wrong. On the morning of March 18, 1676, daylight revealed to those still in the garrison John Wickes's head atop a pole planted in front of the house. Two volunteers cautiously removed it and buried it nearby. Several days later, his mutilated torso was found in a bramble thicket. Without opening the first grave, a second, longer one was dug next to it and Wickes's decapitated body was buried there. Considering the circumstances under which his remains lie in those two separate graves, it would undoubtedly be quite correct to say that John Wickes was buried head first.

Drum Rock is a huge boulder in a field at the end of Drum Rock Road. Though it weighs about two and one-half tons, it can be rocked on its base to produce a drumming sound. Indians used that sound as a warning signal in times of danger.

Rocky Point is in Warwick. What is today a public beach was just a barren shore when that gustatory ceremony we call a clambake was invented there in 1825 by a Bristol schoolteacher named Otis Storrs. Fond of occasionally taking his pupils for an excursion across the bay from Bristol, he anchored at Rocky Point and then discovered he had neglected to bring anything to eat. Storrs was forced to improvise. He directed the girls to gather fruit and berries while the boys kindled a driftwood fire in a rock crevice, heating beach stones that were then covered with damp rockweed. Clams and fish were added and the hatch cover from their sailboat was spread over all. A fabulous finger-food feast followed, and the recipe hasn't changed much since then.

Every state should have at least one haunted house. Rhode Island has one at 1351 Cranston Street in Cranston, on the outskirts of Providence. While the Cranston Print Works still owned the mansion, an apparition was seen descending the stairs in 1925 and a ghost was encountered in the wine cellar. The Sprague Mansion is now the home of the Cranston Historical Society. During the volunteer work in preparing the building for the society, an apparition was seen in the "Doll Room" on the third floor by a member who was so shaken he refused to go upstairs ever again. Just after the society acquired the mansion, a group of teenaged members volunteered to act as resident guards at night. Their nocturnal peace was frequently disturbed by creaks, thumps, and footsteps. One boy, a substitute guard, lasted only a single night. A light mysteriously clicked on in the Doll Room, and he went up and turned it off. As soon as he returned downstairs, it clicked on again. After this happened a few more times, he abandoned his post and never returned.

In 1852, Rhode Island abolished the death penalty because of an event that involved the Sprague Mansion, built by a certain William Sprague in 1790 and inherited by his two sons. While one son went into politics (and later became a Rhode Island governor and then U.S. senator), the other, Amasa Sprague, stayed at the mansion and ran the Sprague business empire. Strongly opposed to drinking and card playing, Amasa quarreled with three Gordon brothers and blocked their efforts to obtain a license to sell liquor in their store. Amasa was later found brutally murdered on his own land, disabled by a gunshot wound and then beaten to death. The Gordon brothers were arrested. Two had alibis but the third Gordon was convicted and executed. At a later time, one of the other Gordons made a deathbed confession that he had been the murderer, not his executed brother. Shocked by the miscarriage of justice his confession had exposed, the Rhode Island legislature abolished the death penalty for all time.

Before heading into Providence, a side trip northwest of Cranston might be of interest. North Scituate is on Route 116 just south of U.S. 6. The Scituate Congregational Church there has two unusual architectural features, one being that the floor slopes upward from where the preacher stood. At the rear of the congregation, the floor is sixteen inches higher than at the front. Since all pew fees were about equal, this feature allowed those in the rear to see and hear as well as those in the front. The other feature is responsible for the church being known as the "church with the backward pews." Built in 1830, all of its pews are placed facing the two front doors. The choir sat behind the congregation and only the minister, on his platform in front of the pews, and the organist, facing the choir, had their backs to the doors. The popular—and well publicized—explanation is that the congregation sat facing the doors so they could watch for a surprise Indian attack. However, Indian raids were no longer a threat when the church was built. One story uses the British and the War of 1812 as the reason—but again, the church didn't even exist then. What seems to be a more valid theory is that the pews were placed so that the assembled congregation, including those with a good view though seated at the back, could stare at every latecomer. Late entry before the somber glare of those already gathered for worship would be a social embarrassment to habitual stragglers. (In 1675 Massachusetts law required the locking of church doors during services because too many people were leaving before the long sermons were over.) Perhaps tardy worshipers eventually preferred total absence to late arrival, because church attendance declined by the end of the century, and in 1940 the building was deeded to the town to be used exclusively for religious or historical purposes.

Still farther northwest, where U.S. 44 and Route 102 cross, is Chepachet, famous for at least one major event in Rhode Island history, the Dorr War of 1842. A monument to that episode lies inside Chepachet Cemetery. To visit it, enter the cemetery, drive to its highest point, and then walk down a worn path to the large boulder in a glade at the bottom. The hill is Acote Hill and the boulder monument is dedicated to Thomas W. Dorr, who was for a brief time the outlaw governor of Rhode Island. In 1842 the Royal Charter of 1663 was Rhode Island's governing document. Because of its property requirements, fully half of the adult male population was not allowed to vote. Reform efforts failed. Thomas Dorr founded a People's party, which held an extralegal constitutional convention and then passed a referendum ratifying a new constitution. When Dorr was elected under the new constitution, Rhode Island had two governors and two constitutions. The established government began arresting Dorr's followers. Dorr planned to resist with the five hundred armed supporters who were pledged to meet at Acote Hill. Only fifty appeared. Although Dorr withdrew, government troops stormed Acote Hill to demonstrate their control over the situation. In that brief martial display, the single casualty was a cow. Dorr was imprisoned for a year but won the final battle when a legal constitutional convention, held later in 1842, approved many of his voting reforms while drawing up a new state constitution by which Rhode Island was governed for many years.

A lesser-known oddity in Chepachet is the Brown and Hopkins Country Store at 1179 Putnam Pike (which seems to be Chepachet's major street). Despite claims from other parts of New England, this is the nation's oldest continuously operated general store, dating from 1809. It still sells groceries as well as antiques, furnishings, gourmet food, and penny candy. You can step right into the past from the sidewalk in front of it. The roll-top desk near the front door has been there since the Civil War era. Antiques are displayed on the second and third floors. If you are hunting for more history, the Glocester Historical Society is housed right next door.

Traveling eastward on U.S. 44 will take you back to Providence. The Rhode Island State Capitol at 82 Smith Street is an architectural landmark constructed of white Georgian marble. Its unusual dome is among the four largest self-supporting domes in the world, the other three being the domes of Saint Peter's in Vatican City, the Taj Mahal in India, and the Minnesota State Capitol in Saint Paul. Another oddity is the "Gettysburg Gun" near the north portico. Just before Gen. George Pickett's charge at Gettysburg, the gun was struck by a rebel shell, killing the two cannoneers who were reloading it. The muzzle of the gun was altered by the shell. Efforts to reload it with a new shot were futile, despite the use of a hammer and ax. The shot became firmly wedged in the barrel, where it remains today.

The Arcade is the nation's first indoor shopping mall. Built of granite in 1828 (when Providence's population was only fourteen thousand souls), the 216-foot structure fronts on both Westminster and Weybosset streets. It's one of the finest examples of Greek Revival architecture in America, with six massive granite columns at each entrance that were the largest monolithic columns in the country at the time. A glass skylight, supported by wooden beams, illuminates the open area between the three floors. Shops on the second and third levels are connected by long, open balconies overlooking the ground-floor areaway. The building has survived a fire, three hurricane floodings, and the threat of demolition. The Arcade is a national historic landmark that the Metropolitan Museum of Art considers one of the three finest commercial buildings in nineteenth-century American architecture.

A ten-foot statue of Roger Williams stands on Prospect Terrace overlooking Providence. No one knows exactly what Roger Williams looked like, but the statue is a monument to the man who founded Rhode Island on the principle of religious freedom. According to information provided to visitors, Roger Williams is buried right there, but in fact, most of Roger Williams is not buried anywhere. He died in 1683 and was interred with honors by the town in a spot close to his home. The grave was unmarked, but when one of his descendants was buried nearby in 1739, the diggers accidentally uncovered one end of Roger Williams's coffin. A small boy was lowered into the new grave to investigate, and he reported that the root of an apple tree had grown into the interior of the coffin. The grave remained unmarked and undisturbed until March 22, 1860, when a descendant requested that it be opened. At this point accounts of what was found in the coffin begin to differ. Dust, rusty nails, loam, decayed wood, or braided hair appeared in various reports, though only one mentioned a few small bones. They all agreed, however, that within the coffin was a long apple tree root.

During the long years that had passed since his grave was accidentally opened, the tree root had continued to grow. By 1860 it had followed his body down to the thighs, where it divided, one branch following each leg to its foot. An additional root at one side apparently followed one arm and hand. To some viewers, the knees and feet are easily distinguishable in the root. You can judge for yourself by visiting the Rhode Island Historical Society Museum, where the roots are on display.

Some small part of Roger Williams may be buried in a bronze box under his memorial. What happened to the rest of him? Apple tree roots consume everything organic in their path, including phosphates from bones, so the answer lies in whatever happened to the apples he apparently nourished. Cider, anyone?

To get to the Slater Mill Historic Site in Pawtucket, take Exit 28 off I-95, then turn left, cross the bridge, and follow the signs. It was here that America's Industrial Revolution began. In the 1780s, when England was trying to protect its textile monopoly by preventing information about textile machinery from leaving England, Samuel Slater is said to have memorized the entire mechanism of the water-powered spinning and carding machines used there, and then smuggled that technology out of the country to America in 1789 to build similar machines from memory. The truth is less romantic. As an indentured apprentice in England, Slater did learn a great deal about the machinery. However, he was known to be a textile worker, and when he left England, he openly carried his indenture papers to demonstrate his skills to future employers. As for his legendary memory, it took Slater several years and the skills of many assistants before he finally constructed similar machinery in America.

Slater was truly the father of our manufacturing industry. His real claim to fame lay in his managerial skills. He created the first "company town." Once his mill was up and running, he organized an entire community to operate it. He created mill villages across southern New England and a system of labor using entire families. After building a mill, he organized housing, stores, schools, and churches, so the entire life of the town centered around his mill. In a period when children were often exploited, Slater offered to provide schooling at his own expense. His offer was not matched by other employers but his industrial methods were scrutinized and copied.

Dr. William P. Rothwell is buried in Pawtucket's Oak Grove Cemetery. A convivial man who hated the thought that friends would mourn his death, Dr. Rothwell had a large boulder transported from his summer home and placed on top of his burial plot. To remind people of his sociable nature and inspire them to laugh rather than weep at his memory, Rothwell had the following statement engraved on the boulder: "This Is On Me."

From Pawtucket, it is easy to head south to I-195 and then southeast to the Fall River area. Exit onto Route 24 westward (or south) and then switch to Route 81 south. At the end of 81 you'll be in Adamsville, which has two oddities in the center of town. One is the Rhode Island Red Commemorative Monument—a pointed granite stone monument to a chicken. Rhode Island Red hens were developed in this area. Poultry experiments were begun in 1854 by Capt. William Tripp of Little Compton and John Macomber. First they crossed Malay and Java cocks with Cochin China hens. The resulting breed was then crossed with Light Brahmas, Plymouth Rocks, and Brown Leghorns. The final breed was the Rhode Island

Red, which had a high egg yield and still made a delicious meal. It was recognized as a legitimate breed at the Providence poultry show in 1895 and is a distinctive Rhode Island contribution to our dinner tables.

A few yards away from the monument is the "Spite Tower," a tall structure, tapering in toward the top like a four-sided lighthouse. It stands squarely between a store and a house just down the street. You can select from a small menu of legends as to why the tower was built that way and in that location. One says it was the result of unrequited love and was built to block out a view of the store where the woman worked. Another claims that it was built out of revenge because the builder's wife had not received a

Spite Tower

bequest that had been deeded to the woman in the store. Perhaps it was built simply to utilize its water source, a deep spring-fed well. The best of the myths involves John Hathaway, who lived in the house and built the tower. The storekeeper, Abe Manchester, slept above the store but took his meals at Hathaway's house. A towel was hung from a window as a signal to Abe when his meal was ready. The two friends had a falling out and Hathaway then built the tower so Abe couldn't see the signal. Although they later renewed their friendship, the tower remained.

Little Compton is southwest of Adamsville along country roads. The original Indian name meant "the black goose comes." Not much there to attract wandering travelers, except for the Commons Burying Ground. Elizabeth Pabodie is buried there in the thirtieth row. Her father was John Alden. When Miles Standish was courting Priscilla Mullins in the Plymouth colony, he asked John Alden to put in a good word with her on his behalf. He did so but Priscilla replied, "Speak for yourself, John." He did, and they were married, and in 1623 their first child, Elizabeth, was the first child known to have been born of white settlers in New England. She became Elizabeth Pabodie by marrying William Pabodie in 1644. She lived ninety-four years, and at her death in 1717 she had over five hundred living descendants.

In the twenty-seventh row of the Commons Burying Ground is the grave of Elizabeth Palmer, who had married Simeon Palmer in 1755 and was his second wife. Her epitaph, presumably written by her husband, is mysterious:

> *In memory of Elizabeth who should have been the wife of Mr. Simeon Palmer who died August 14th, 1776 in the 64th year of her age.*

Why did he imply they hadn't been married? One local tale is that Simeon was a parsimonious man of such difficult disposition that from their wedding night on, they lived separate lives, with Elizabeth confining her wifely duties to mending his clothes and cooking his meals. However, they did have a child and Elizabeth named her Lydia, the name of Simeon's first wife. Perhaps that supports a more romantic legend in which young Simeon decided during a lengthy sea voyage that he wanted to marry Elizabeth and sent her an elaborately written proposal by a shipmate returning to Little Compton. Unfortunately, the proposal was never delivered. When Simeon returned home, believing himself rejected because he had received no answer, he hastily married Lydia Dennis before he learned the truth. After Lydia's death, Simeon and Elizabeth were united at last.

Ocean-Born Mary grew up in a Londonderry, New Hampshire, house that had been built in 1730. (For her full story, see page 39.) More than two hundred years later, that house was dismantled and then reassembled in Little Compton. A shingled, gambrel-roof cottage with a large center chimney, it is known locally as the "Seaborn Mary" House.

By driving north from Little Compton on Route 77 to Tiverton, one passes over Sin and Flesh Brook, which received its name after King Philip's warriors caught Zoeth Holland on a nearby granite outcropping, whereupon they killed him and threw his dismembered body into the brook. Continuing north into Bristol, the really curious can visit the remote spot where King Philip finally died. (Follow signs to the Haffenreffer Museum of Anthropology on Tower Road. Staff members can direct you to the specific location.) Though King Philip's War ravaged much of New England, King Philip's power base was at a spring near the museum. When the war went against him, he secretly retreated there. Benjamin Church, who believed the war could be ended only by King Philip's death, hunted him in vain. Unfortunately, the warlike Philip had earlier killed one of his own Indians for urging that Philip make peace with the settlers. That Indian's brother, Alderman, obtained his revenge by telling Church where Philip was hiding. With Alderman as a guide, Church led a small party in a surprise raid. Philip, who once predicted he would never be killed by a white man, tried to escape into Mirey Swamp but was shot by Alderman. Philip's body was dismembered and scattered. His head, however, was taken to Plymouth and displayed there on a pole for twenty years. One of King Philip's hands was awarded to Alderman as a trophy. In later years he often exhibited Philip's hand immersed in a bucket of rum. A rectangular boulder now marks the location where Philip's war ended. Placed there in 1877, it is inscribed: "In the 'Miery Swamp' 165 feet W.S.W. from this spring, according to tradition King Philip fell Aug. 12, 1670 O.S."

Stop in at the Herreshoff Marine Museum and enjoy the classic collection of exhibits about the golden age of yachting. Located where the Herreshoffs designed and built eight consecutive successful America's Cup defenders between 1893 and 1934, their success is even more impressive when you learn that the original designer, John B. Herreshoff, became blind when only fifteen years old. By then he had already obtained such a knowledge and a "feel" for boats that his blindness seemed to be no handicap. In 1863 when he was twenty-two, he fitted up an old tannery, bought seasoned supplies, and hired a work crew. Blessed with an exceptional photographic memory, he dictated specifications to his brother Nathanael, who used them to construct a model yacht. By carefully feeling the model, John used his uncanny intuition to note defects and suggest improvements. He could also estimate building costs down to the last dollar.

Along with their yachting accomplishments, the Herreshoffs seem to have invented baking powder, paint that resisted seaweed and barnacles, superheated steam engines, ankle braces for ice skates, and sliding seats for rowboats. In 1885 they built America's first torpedo boat.

It's not surprising that a native Rhode Islander, Esek Hopkins, was the Continental Navy's first commander, but the army also has a local story. Heading south into Portsmouth on Route 114, look for a merger with Route 24. There a memorial to black soldiers is dedicated to the black companies of the First Rhode Island Battalion, often called the Black Regiment. Popularly believed to be the first black soldiers to defend our country, they fought valiantly against the British in Portsmouth in 1778 during the battle of Rhode Island. Our first black regiment earned a place in history during its gallant stand at the spot now commemorated by a flagpole.

Now look for Cory's Lane (on the right as you head south) and the Green Animals Topiary Gardens. Topiary gardening is the cen-

Green Animals
Topiary Gardens

turies-old art form of fashioning living plants to look like animals or geometric figures, a landscaping technique that used to delight royalty and the landed gentry. In addition to many geometric figures and ornamental designs, Green Animals has twenty-one animals and birds shaped out of California privet and yew. They include a boar, camel, donkey, elephant, giraffe, hen, lion, ostrich, reindeer, rooster, swan, unicorn, two bears, three peacocks, three dogs, and a horse with a rider. The most popular is the teddy bear, between whose widespread paws a child can pose for a photo. Don't overlook the main house, which features original furnishings and Victorian toy collections. The immense copper beech tree on the front lawn is more than 150 years old.

A bit farther south on Route 114, at the southern end of the island the Indians called Aquidneck, the town of Newport draws many visitors today, especially those wishing to view the magnificent opulence of the Newport mansions. (Because of Newport's many attractions, it is wise to avoid visiting on weekends or holidays during the summer season.) And there are other unusual places to visit. The first synagogue in our country was built in New

York in 1728, but the Jeshuat Israel Synagogue on Touro Street is now the oldest Jewish house of worship in America. The first Jewish families arrived in Newport from Holland in 1658. In 1763, after nearly a century of worshiping in their homes, they built the synagogue. Constructed at an acute angle with the street so that the ark could face directly east, its interior is considered an architectural masterpiece. During the days before the Civil War, the synagogue used its quarters as a station on the Underground Railroad when fugitive slaves traveled along that secret avenue to freedom in the North.

Also in Newport is America's oldest continuously operating tavern. The building that became the White Horse Tavern in 1687 was actually constructed as early as 1673 by William Mayes, father of the famous pirate with the same name who eventually gave up piracy to join his father as a landlord. Both the general assembly and the criminal court have held sessions in the White Horse Tavern. Today huge fireplaces, exposed beams, and many oil portraits provide a setting for elegant and formal dining either in the tap room or in several dining rooms.

In New England's naval history, many seafarers became privateers and many of those became pirates. Twenty-six pirates were convicted and hanged near Newport's Long Wharf on July 19, 1723. They were buried somewhere between the high and low water marks on Goat Island, outside Newport Harbor. Strangely enough, that event also brought an end to the criminal career of Rhode Island's most successful counterfeiter, Mary Butterworth. Counterfeiting was a relatively new crime; the printing of paper money had only been permitted since around the turn of the century. In 1705 Thomas Odell was sentenced in Boston for counterfeiting Massachusetts paper money, which had just been issued. Mary Butterworth started ten years later but she lasted much longer. Instead of printing from metal plates (which could not be destroyed in a hurry and if discovered would be sufficient evidence to convict her), she devised an ingenious printing system using simple household skills and materials. She would wet a piece of muslin, place it on top of a legal bill of credit, and press down with a flatiron, transferring the bill's image to the muslin. While the muslin was still damp, she would slip a piece of precut paper under it and press down again. The bill's image appeared on the paper, faint but accurate. With a quill pen and printer's ink, she traced the faint outlines until she had a convincing counterfeit bill. Evidence of her criminal technique disappeared when she tossed the muslin into the fire.

For eight years Mary Butterworth printed "funny money" in her kitchen without detection. To pass the phony bills, she selected her agents carefully. Eleven trusted accomplices traveled about New England, passing off her counterfeit bills to unsuspecting merchants. Ultimately Rhode Island was forced to recall a legally issued series of five-pound notes. However, one accomplice, Arthur Noble, could not resist being present in Newport to watch the mass hanging of pirates. Running into some old friends, he decided to celebrate the grisly event with them. He paid for the party with a forged bill, and a sharp-eyed waitress called the constables. Noble kept his mouth shut, but an associate confessed, prompting the constables to swoop down on Mary Butterworth's kitchen. She was arrested and jailed on August 15, 1723, but all the constables found was a flatiron, paper, muslin, ink, and pens—and no counterfeiting plates. Mary Butterworth walked free.

Brenton Point is at the extreme southern end of Newport. Brenton's Reef, a short distance out of Newport Harbor, is a perilous location where many ships came to grief. Jahleel Brenton, a prominent Tory during the revolution, often entertained British officers in his home on the Point. On one such occasion, a Lieutenant Stanley spent some time staring at Brenton's adopted daughter Alice, whom Brenton had rescued as the sole survivor of a wreck on Brenton's Reef. When Lieutenant Stanley was questioned about his interest in Alice, he explained that she bore a striking resemblance to his own younger sister, who had left England years before and had been lost at sea. Further inquiry revealed that Alice was indeed that younger sister, Beatrice Stanley.

For the connoisseur of gravestones, Newport has several oddities. In the Common Burying Ground is the grave of Newport's beloved Ida Lewis, a female lighthouse keeper who, for more than fifty years, braved the turbulent waters off Lime Rock to save about forty people from drowning, among them boaters, swimmers, drunken sailors, and even a sheep. The Lime Rock Light, where she lived, is on an island only 250 yards from the mainland. In her honor it has been renamed the Ida Lewis Yacht Club, probably the only club of its kind in America named for a woman. In her epitaph she is described as "the grace darling of America." The same cemetery has an inscription about James Anthony, who "spent his life upon the sea, fighting for the nation. He doubled his enjoyment by doubling all his rations." In the Island Cemetery (just over the fence from the Common Burying Ground) is a grave with this epitaph:

> *My Friend, Jack Hammett, The Best of Dogs. Aged 11 Years.*
> *In life ever at my side, always ready to comfort and protect me,*
> *Dying at my feet in his old age, he now rests beside the one he*
> *loved.*

Jack is buried next to the grave of Capt. Mathias Marin, which is marked with an immense anchor of polished marble.

Newport encourages visitors to wander through its sumptuous

Norse tower

mansions, many of which offer guided tours to the public, and to gaze with awe at the lavish surroundings. However, one of the least impressive structures in town may be the most controversial building in America. Known either as the "old stone mill" or the "Norse tower," the squat, drumlike structure supported by eight legs stands in a small park. It is made of lime-mortared fieldstone, is twenty-six feet high, and lacks a roof. Arches separate the legs, and small square openings are scattered in the wall above them. The puzzle is that no one knows for certain when it was built or by whom. Of the two mainstream theories, the simpler one is that the tower was of colonial construction. A familiar sight since at least 1675, it may have been constructed by Gov. Benedict Arnold (great-grandfather of the patriot/traitor). The belief is that when a windmill belonging to Peter Easton was blown down in a hurricane, Governor Arnold constructed another windmill to replace it. Support for the theory comes from Arnold's 1677 will in which he refers to "my stone-built windmiln."

Not so, say those who claim that the tower was built by Vikings. They point out that although Arnold may have used it as a windmill, there is no proof anywhere that he built it. Perhaps he only adapted an ancient ruin to a timely use. If he built it, why doesn't that fact appear anywhere in the town records? This negative view is matched by some positive evidence. During speculations about Vikings exploring New England coasts, similarities were noted between the stone tower and early church buildings in Europe, leading to the conclusion that the tower had originally been a Viking church.

Someone pointed out that near the place in England where Arnold was born and brought up stood the Chesterton windmill, very similar in appearance to the Newport tower. Someone else then revealed that Arnold had actually been born a hundred miles away from the Chesterfield mill and that it had been built as an observatory only two years before Arnold left England and was not converted to a mill until long after Arnold died. The Viking enthusiasts mentioned that the Newport tower was oriented to the true points of the compass as were churches in Denmark and Norway.

The great debate continued, new evidence to support one theory being countered by evidence to support the other. Then an archaeological project seemed finally to have resolved the controversy. When diggers located the trench ringing the structure (originally dug to receive the footings for the tower), they uncovered colonial artifacts at the bottom and under some of the columns. The adherents of Norse priority countered with the claim that an ambulatory wall surrounding the tower was missed by the diggers and that the archaeological excavation simply uncovered a doorway in the wall that the colonists had later used themselves. That will remain unproved unless the park commission reverses its ban against future excavations. And so it goes. In a town that promoted religious freedom while it also became a leader in the slave trade and in which the rich owners of mansions referred to local citizens as their "footstools," the ambiguity of that stone tower may make it Newport's most appropriate symbol.

It would take 488 Rhode Islands to fit inside Alaska, our largest state. However, more people live in Providence alone than in all of Alaska! Our smallest state has never hesitated to march to its own drummer. In 1647 marriages by self-agreement betrothal (which were common among Quakers) were outlawed in Rhode Island. When one woman who had lived with her "husband" for twenty years petitioned for separation, she was stigmatized, fined, and ordered "not to lead soe scandalose life." After a few performances of *Othello* were staged in 1761, the Rhode Island Assembly enacted legislation barring such theatrical exhibitions, with a penalty of one hundred pounds for each actor.

Rhode Island was the first American colony to declare independence from Great Britain, and the last of the original thirteen to surrender its freedom by joining the United States. No wonder the statue standing on top of the state capitol is known as *The Independent Man.*

CONNECTICUT

The original spelling for this state was "Quinnehtukqut," an Indian word meaning "beside the long tidal river." Connecticut calls itself the Constitution State because the Fundamental Orders it adopted in 1638–39 was the basis for its constitution, making it the first of the thirteen colonies to draft one. No one knows what to call people who live there, although "commuters" seems an appropriate suggestion. Informally it's the Nutmeg State, because colonial peddlers sometimes sold small wooden knobs to spice-hungry housewives, falsely claiming the knobs were nutmegs.

Fairfield is along I-95 up the coast from the New York area, and at first glance, two gravestones there might make you wonder if con artists are still at work. Its Old Burying Ground is on Beach Road near the town center and south of the village green. This attractive, unusually well maintained cemetery was created in 1687 and contains the graves of more than one hundred Revolutionary soldiers. Not far from the main entrance are two adjacent gravestones— both for Abigail Squier, wife of Samuel Squier. The only apparent difference between them is a five-year discrepancy in the death dates. Closer scrutiny makes it clear that Samuel Squier's first wife was named Abigail, and after she died, Samuel Squier married a second Abigail, who lived five years longer than had the first Abigail. There is a barely noticeable "2d" before the word *Wife* on the younger tombstone. Samuel seems not to have distinguished between them in his memorial epitaphs to both, which isn't too surprising when you consider his own epitaph; it bears the inscription "Praises on tombstones are but vainly spent."

Beyond Fairfield is Bridgeport, with its unique example of how the old and the new can be mixed. The HMS *Rose* was a British frigate, active in both the Seven Years War and the American Revolution. Built in 1757 to fight during the French and Indian Wars, it was scuttled across the river channel outside Savannah, Georgia, in 1779 to prevent the French fleet from approaching that city. The present *Rose* was built in 1970 from the original plans and is a full-rigged training ship berthed at Captain's Cove in Bridgeport. All 13,000 square feet of her 17 sails are 100 percent polyester, recycled from plastic car fenders and more than 126,000 plastic soda bottles. Today's *Rose* is the largest active Tall Ship in the world, and those who pay to voyage aboard her are not merely passengers but participants who may wind up furling sails, bracing the yards on a starboard tack, or taking a turn at the helm. Please, no radios, tape players, or loud electronic devices.

Remember knock-knock jokes? Up the coast from Bridgeport, the 1850 phenomenon known as the "Stratford Knockings" was no laughing matter. Stratford was settled in 1639 and named after England's Stratford-upon-Avon, Shakespeare's birthplace. Its sturdy populace engaged in shipbuilding and oyster fishing. America's first white centenarian was buried there in 1698. In 1649, to escape a public lashing, a Milford man sought refuge in Stratford by swimming across the Housatonic River. He had broken the blue laws by kissing his wife on Sunday. Joined later by his family, he became one of Stratford's leading citizens. Stratford was a solid, reliable, down-to-earth town.

In 1849 Reverend Eliakim Phelps purchased a three-story Greek Revival frame house on Stratford's prestigious Elm Street. He moved in with his bride, a former widow, and her four children, ages three to sixteen. On the morning of March 10, 1850, Dr.

Phelps and his wife returned from Sunday church service. Fastened by the front door, a piece of black crepe fluttered in the breeze. When they entered, they saw that various articles of furniture had been upset and strewn around. Accounts differ as to what else they saw. Some say that in one of the main downstairs rooms, a dummy of a human figure was laid out for burial. Others say that eleven female dummies were posed in attitudes of prayer and in their midst hung the dummy of a hideous dwarf. From that day on, the house was besieged by unnatural happenings. Rappings and thumpings were followed by sharp knocks on headboards, ceilings, and floors. Occasionally, loud crashes were heard in various unoccupied rooms. Objects flew through the air. Property damage was considerable.

The Stratford knockings lasted for seven months, attracting supernaturalists, skeptics, reporters, and editors. Always welcomed by Dr. Phelps and invited to stay overnight for a closer study of the happenings, the investigators came and went, some of them having been given special attention by the unseen forces. Unable to explain the occurrences and unwilling to accept them as supernatural, the experts (and the merely curious) eventually departed. So did Dr. Phelps, who finally moved his family to Philadelphia. The house on Elm Street became peaceful, leading some skeptics to conclude that the mischievous children had been responsible for the manifestations.

In the late 1940s, two strange events occurred in that same house, which had been converted into a convalescent home with a three-floor buzzer system. One buzzer was on the top floor, the living quarters for the two owners and their two-and-a-half-year-old son Gary. That buzzer was mounted on a wall beyond the reach of Gary, who slept in a crib and was too small to climb out of it. One night the buzzer sounded while the owners were in the basement. As they rushed upstairs, they smelled smoke and heard Gary scream. A blanket had accidentally caught fire and was smoldering. The owners never learned what set off the buzzer. About two years later, the buzzer sounded a similar warning. By then Gary slept in a bed in his own room. Shortly after midnight Gary's mother, who was on duty on the main floor, heard the third floor buzzer. Hurrying to answer it, she looked up when she reached the second floor and saw sleepwalking Gary about to climb over the railing at the top of the three-story stairwell. She grabbed him before he fell. Again, no one ever learned what had activated the buzzer. As far as Gary's parents were concerned, "If there's a ghost in that house, it was a good ghost. When we moved out, it was like leaving a friend." The Phelps mansion, vandalized and abandoned, was torn down in the 1950s. But there's a rumor that if you walk along Elm Street in a late night fog, the ghostly home of the Stratford knockings is sometimes vaguely visible through the murky mist.

Beyond Stratford is Milford and the Milford Cemetery—with an epitaph not for the squeamish. In the southeast corner by the tracks is the grave of Miss Mary Fowler, who died in 1792 at the young age of twenty-four. On her slate gravestone is:

> *Molly tho pleasant in her day*
> *Was sudd'nly seiz'd and sent away*
> *How soon shes ripe how soon shes rott'n*
> *Sent to her grave, & soon forgott'n.*

A similar verse used to be seen in the Doolittle Cemetery in Hamden above the grave of Milla Gaylord, but that tombstone was stolen some years ago.

Still farther up the coast, New Haven boasts a rather extensive collection of historical oddities. The world's first telephone switchboard, made of bustle wire and pot handles, was created in New Haven. Charles Goodyear invented vulcanized rubber there, inspired by a New York shopkeeper who told him a fortune could be made by anyone who discovered how to keep rubber from sticking or softening in the sun. A New Haven magician invented the automobile self-starter. And the lollipop was born when candy was placed on a stick in New Haven. The Colt revolver was invented and produced at New Haven's Whitney Armory in 1836. In New Haven, David Bushnell invented his "squadron of kegs"—floating mines that were used against the British in New London Harbor and in the Delaware off Philadelphia.

Two of the unusual firsts in New Haven are culinary. Naples,

Italy, is the source of pizza as we now know it. But even prior to
A.D. 1000, a flat bread served with herbs and spices called "apizza"
was being eaten there. (The tomato was added after it became popular in Europe during the nineteenth century.) Frank Pepe introduced pizza to America in 1925, when he began selling pies from a
horse-drawn cart in New Haven. Even more remarkable to oddity
hunters is Louis' Lunch, which still exists on Crown Street between
College and High streets. In 1900 it was small luncheonette run by
Louis Lassen in a different location. He began making patties out
of the trimmings from his famous steak sandwiches and grilling
them with a thin slice of onion. One day someone in a hurry dashed
in and asked Louis for a quick meal he could eat on the run. Louis
hastily sandwiched a broiled beef patty between two chunks of
toast and sent the customer on his way with America's first ham-
burger. For generations Louis' Lunch filled a special niche in the
hearts of New Haveners. When the diner was threatened with
demolition to make way for a new high rise, scores of people acted
to preserve the luncheonette. Hours before its planned destruction,
this small landmark was shifted to its present location. To help in
its restoration, thousands of bricks came from all parts of the
world; a "tour of the walls" is now available for special customers.
Not much else has changed at Louis' Lunch. His historic ham-
burger is still the house specialty—freshly ground beef broiled ver-
tically in the original cast iron grill and served between slices of
toast. Cheese, tomato, and onion are Louis' standard garnishes, but
mustard and ketchup are classed as corruptions. Indeed, all of
America is indebted to New Haven for our two most popular
foods.

Anyone attempting to kill a dictator, a president, or an emperor
is simply an assassin. Those attempting to kill a king have a special
label: "regicides." In 1661 two regicides lived intermittently in a
New Haven cave now known as the "Judges' Cave." It doesn't look
much like a cave anymore, but three standing stones mark its location in the Hamden section of the West Rock Ridge State Park. A
tablet there concludes with, "Opposition to tyrants is obedience to
God."

What brought the two regicides there began when Oliver Cromwell defeated the royalist armies of King Charles I in England. The Court of Commissioners tried King Charles and sentenced him to death. Fifty-nine of the sixty-seven Commissioners signed the death warrant, and when Charles I was beheaded on January 30, 1649, those who had signed became regicides. Royalty returned in 1660 with Charles II determined to get revenge. Now classed as traitors to the Crown, only thirty-six regicides were still alive. Thirteen escaped from England and two of them, Edward Whalley and William Goffe, sought refuge in Boston. Their presence was no big secret. They were well-received by Governor John Endecott and other notables. However, when notice of those who had been granted indemnity arrived in November and their names were not included, the fugitives moved eastward to friendly protectors in New Haven. The hunt was on. One hundred pounds had been offered for their capture, dead or alive. Whalley and Goffe disappeared from public view.

Bounty hunters sent from England with royal warrants were baffled by delays and subterfuges. In a letter from New Haven officials to Boston claiming that the fugitives had gone, one ingenious sentence is 229 words long but virtually meaningless. For more than three years Whalley and Goffe remained hidden in the New Haven area, sometimes in cellars, at times in private homes, often in the woods, and several times in the "Judges' Cave." They lived in that cave from May 15 until June 11, supplied daily with food by Richard Sperry, who lived nearby. Food was placed in a basin and tied up in a cloth. Sperry occasionally asked one of his boys to deliver it by leaving it on a certain stump. When the empty basin was recovered, the curious boy was simply told by his father that someone working in the woods needed the food. Worried that their continued presence constituted a threat to the safety of their friends, Whalley and Goffe moved on to Hadley in October. They remained in close hiding for more than a dozen years. Whalley died around 1675 and Goffe disappeared around 1678. The exact circumstances of their deaths and burials are not known. What is absolutely certain is that Charles II never caught up with the two regicides who had lived for a time in the Judges' Cave.

While in the Hamden area, visitors should take the time to visit

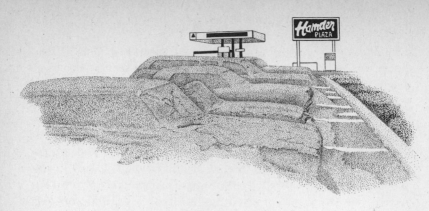

Ghost parking lot

the Hamden Plaza Shopping Center on Dixwell Avenue. It made its debut in 1955 as the first shopping center in the region. Public controversy about it arose in 1978 when its "ghost parking lot" created a stir among the locals. A group of twenty discarded vehicles had been stripped, sandblasted, and covered with concrete. Lined up in a row at various levels facing Dixwell Avenue, they were then sprayed with a thick coating of asphalt that flowed down into the surrounding paving, creating the impression that the cars were attempting to rise up from below the macadam. Why were they there? Officially, "The concept deals with a number of factors characteristic of the American mobilized experience—the blurred vision of motion itself, the fetishism of the car, interdeterminacy of place and object. . . ." and so on. Bizarre rumors began to circulate about the cars, such as that they had all been involved in fatal accidents. Such stories satisfied the artist, whose real motive was to draw attention to the shopping plaza and to create a little controversy about it. After all, what better symbol could one choose for a shopping center? Without cars, they wouldn't exist.

Heading north on I-91 out of Hamden, take Exit 15 onto Route 68 and detour east a short way to Durham. New England's oldest operating water supply company, the Durham Aqueduct Company, was started there on February 22, 1798, when nineteen residents created a water system to supply their homes from a nearby spring. Water was fed by gravity to twelve homes on Main Street and one on Maiden Lane, which also might make it the smallest such company. Sometime after beginning operation, the company's supply pipes became clogged with silt. A good-size eel was procured and inserted backward into the water system's pipe at the upper end. When a plug at the lower end was removed, water flowed downstream while the eel tried valiantly to swim upstream. The eel was washed backward all the way down the pipe, pushing the accumulated sediment behind him. The eel survived, and the water flowed freely again.

Continuing north on I-91, a short side trip west on Route 9 will take you to East Berlin, where you will find Connecticut perfectly centered beneath your feet: you will be standing at the exact geographic center of the state. There's still another reason for being in that neighborhood. Berlin is just next door, and adjacent to its Kensington Congregational Church (on Route 71 south of Berlin's Main Street) stands a Civil War memorial that is the oldest one in the state, probably the oldest one in New England, and possibly the oldest one in America. The death rate of Berlin soldiers was very high; more than half of the men it sent to the Sixteenth Connecticut Regiment of Infantry perished. This plain brownstone shaft was dedicated on July 25, 1863, two years before the war ended.

Dinosaur State Park is in Rocky Hill, just a step farther north on I-91 and one mile east of Exit 23. It seems like an odd name for a New England park. After all, dinosaur bones are usually found in our western states or in remote corners of the world like Mongolia. (Mongolia is where the first velociraptor skeleton was recently found, and that dinosaur was the vicious killer in the movie *Jurassic Park*.) But dinosaurs in the Connecticut River valley? Not any more, of course, yet the area once teemed with them. Roughly 300 million years ago, dinosaurs thrived in this fossil-rich valley. When their age came to an end, the tracks they left in the Triassic mud were slowly buried and preserved by layers of tidal sediment. Dinosaur tracks can be seen today as far north as Smith's Ferry and South Hadley in Massachusetts.

Dinosaur State Park has an unusual trackway where visitors can literally follow in the footsteps of the dinosaurs. Almost fifteen hundred tracks were accidentally uncovered in 1966 and buried again to preserve them. A year later five hundred more dinosaur tracks dating to the Jurassic period were discovered, and these are now covered by the Exhibit Center's geodesic dome. Exactly which dinosaur species made the tracks is still undetermined. The skeletal remains that best match the tracks and the spacing between them is the Dilophosaurus, a carnivorous beast. Take a look at the park's twenty-foot-long reconstruction of this flesh eater and be happy it's not around anymore.

The real oddity in this state park is that they will let you take home a memento of the tracks. Within posted hours from May 1 to October 31, park officials will allow you to make your own plaster cast of a genuine Jurassic dinosaur track. What a paperweight! All you have to do is bring some material yourself—cooking oil, cloth rags, paper towels, a large plastic bucket, and ten pounds of plaster of Paris. Contact park officials for specific information.

Wethersfield, a town of about twenty-six thousand, lies just south of Hartford. A pleasant place to linger, but aside from the fact that it was the first settlement in Connecticut, one might be hard-pressed to find anything really unusual about the town. However, the famous scientist and prolific writer Arthur C. Clarke once said that "the most incredible event I have ever heard of" took place there. He was talking about meteors. Our earth is constantly dinged by meteorites—a large one is still lodged under Chicago's O'Hare International Airport. Most meteors entering our atmosphere never land; they are so tiny that they vaporize while still in the air. It is estimated that only about five hundred actually hit Earth each year, and of these, only ten are recovered, since most meteors fall and sink into the oceans. Obviously, the odds of any small town being hit are pretty low—in fact it is almost unheard of. However, a meteor did hit Wethersfield on April 8, 1971. What's left of it is preserved in the Smithsonian Institution. What's really odd is that eleven years later, Wethersfield was hit by a second meteor (the event that excited Arthur Clarke). It didn't please the chamber of commerce, which doesn't publicize the unusual attraction Wethersfield seems to hold for outerspace bombardment.

East of Wethersfield and across the river from Rocky Hill is Glastonbury. The Rocky Hill–Glastonbury Ferry linking Route 160 west of the river and its continuation on the east side, is the nation's oldest continuously operating ferry service. For centuries, ferries were the only means of crossing the Connecticut River. Back in 1655 this ferry was actually a raft, poled back and forth. Later a horse on a treadmill in the center of the ferry supplied the power to move it. In 1875, steam power replaced the horse power. Today the ferry is a three-car barge pushed along by a diesel-powered tow-boat. Using it can save you about ten miles of road traffic.

South of Glastonbury, the name "Haddam" becomes quite popular along the east bank of the river. First comes Middle Haddam on Route 51, and then Haddam Neck, followed by Haddam Island and Haddam Meadows state parks. Little Haddam is east of them while East Haddam is farther south. (Where is plain Haddam? Across the river.) Linger long enough in East Haddam and you'll hear the bells tolling from Saint Stephen's Episcopal Church. One of them is said to be the world's oldest church bell, cast in A.D. 815 for a Spanish monastery. When that was destroyed by Napoleon's troops, the bell was salvaged and later sent to New York in a shipment of metal. In 1834, a certain William Pratt claimed the bell and sent it to East Haddam, where it was installed at Saint Stephen's. On the knoll overlooking the cemetery at Saint Stephen's is the small red schoolhouse where Nathan Hale taught in 1773 and 1774, two years before he was hanged by the British as a spy.

The Gillette Castle State Park at Hadlyme, south of East Haddam, should not be bypassed. At the turn of the century (and before Basil Rathbone got a lock on the role), William Gillette was the theatergoers' embodiment of Sherlock Holmes. His portrayal of the great detective brought him international fame and fortune, and in 1913 Gillette decided to build his dream house on Long Island—but a cruise in his houseboat changed that plan. While at anchor in the lee of a rocky projection on the Connecticut River, he became so fascinated with its tree-lined hills and lofty ridges that he abandoned his earlier plan, bought 122 acres, and began building at Hadlyme. Gillette designed everything himself, both inside and out, patterning his plan after a medieval Rhenish fortress. It took five years to build the castle. Walls taper from four feet thick at the base to two feet at the tower. A "hanging" wall between the balcony and bedrooms is suspended from steel girders. The forty-seven hand-carved doors are fastened by wooden puzzle locks, no two alike. Gillette included small openings in some doors for his seventeen cats. (One curious newsman counted sixty images of cats decorating parts of the castle.) Gillette gathered colored bottles from

Sherlock Holmes castle

friends and fastened bits of them to the light fixtures. There are trap doors, hidden mirrors (so he could keep an eye on his guests in order to make an effective entrance), a trick bar that folded out of sight in case Prohibition agents came without invitation, a dining table that rolled on tracks (so everything could be laid out ahead of time and then moved to where the diners were already seated). Trains were Gillette's hobby and he constructed a full-scale railway on the grounds. He loved taking houseguests for a three-mile ride with himself at the throttle. (Though the railroad is gone, some of the roadbed can still be seen.) Concerned about the future of his castle after his death, Gillette specified in his will "that the property did not fall into the hands of some blithering saphead who has no conception of where he is or with what surrounded." His instructions have been carried out, much to the delight of the thousands of visitors who arrive annually.

From April to November, the best way to leave the Gillette Castle is by taking the Chester-Hadlyme Ferry over to the river's west bank. Not only will you enjoy looking back at the castle looming above like a medieval fortress, but you will have the pleasure of knowing you are traveling on the second-oldest continuously operating ferry in Connecticut. Serving passengers since 1769, the Chester-Hadlyme Ferry has been steadily updated since. Today's ferryboat is an open, self-propelled craft that can hold up to nine cars and forty-nine passengers. The trip takes only five well-spent minutes.

Touring south from Chester, you've got to hit Old Saybrook and Saybrook Point. It has been claimed that nautical inventor David Bushnell built the world's first submarine here. Actually, he didn't. The first craft capable of moving about underwater was constructed by Cornelius Drebbel, court engineer for James I of England, who first showed off his invention on the Thames River in 1620. It submerged by allowing water into the hull and rose by pumping it out again. Oars, sealed with gaskets, propelled it clumsily. Lack of a power source to make any submersible truly mobile blocked further development until Bushnell solved the problem. His interest in submarines stemmed from earlier experiments with underwater explosives: he had submerged a wooden container filled with gunpowder and ignited it with a fuse, thereby detonating the first underwater mine. Bushnell's invention wreaked such havoc that Bushnell decided to develop an underwater craft that could explode similar mines when they were fastened to enemy warships.

Bushnell's submarine, the *Turtle*, was an egg-shaped vessel about eight feet long and almost as wide. A single occupant could work a treadle to propel outside paddle wheels, and could look through several small windows for steering. The air supply was enough for one man on a thirty-minute voyage, but an air intake valve could be used when the decks were awash. The *Turtle* could transport a payload of 150 pounds of gunpowder. After successful trials off Saybrook in 1775, the *Turtle* went into action against the British flagship *Eagle*, which was at anchor in New York Harbor. Towed as close to it as possible, the *Turtle* then submerged. Outside its bow was a time bomb equipped with an iron screw for penetrating a wooden hull and holding the bomb in place. The *Turtle* was maneuvered into position. Unbeknownst to the attackers, the *Eagle*'s frame was copper-sheathed, so the bomb could not be fastened. Almost a century later the CSS *Hunley*, a Confederate submarine, successfully used the same technique to ram one hundred pounds of black powder into the Union sloop *Housatonic*, sinking it in Charleston Harbor on February 17, 1864. The modern age of submarine warfare probably began there, but the concept was born in Saybrook.

Cypress Cemetery, which overlooks the bay at Saybrook Point, is quite possibly the only New England cemetery containing a plot of ground in which no one will ever be buried. The ground was donated to the town in 1914 on condition that it never be used for burials. A monument identifies it as the first site of Yale College. Perhaps it is really the second site. Does a college exist where the buildings are located or where the students gather to study? The institution that later became Yale University was originally the Collegiate School of Connecticut. Between 1702 and 1707, the students of that college met for instruction in the home of the Reverend Abraham Pierson in what is now Clinton, Connecticut. Pierson is the acknowledged first rector of Yale University. After buildings were erected at Saybrook, the Collegiate School moved there in 1707. So Saybrook became the official site of the college. The first commencement was held September 13, 1702, when the master of arts degree was conferred upon five graduates—all having previously received their bachelor's degree at Harvard!

Trustees decided to move the college to New Haven in 1716. Saybrook refused to give up without a struggle, storing the textbooks in a fortified house guarded by townsmen. When the entrance was forced, those gathering up the books found that their horses had been freed and their wagons damaged. En route to New Haven with new wagons, they found that planking from larger bridges had been removed and that smaller bridges had been destroyed. Two years later in New Haven, the Collegiate School was renamed Yale College (in honor of its generous donor, Elihu Yale), and it has remained there ever since.

On the east side of the river across from Old Saybrook is Old Lyme. At 303 Ferry Road in Old Lyme is the Nut Museum. You could have recognized it by an eight-foot nutcracker hanging out front until vandals destroyed that in 1994. The museum, housed in a Victorian mansion set among nut trees, is probably the only museum in the world dedicated to the uses and origins of nuts. Art is combined with history and lore; the exhibits include paintings, hookings, ceramics, belts, dresses, and illustrations, all pertaining to nuts.

Norwich can be reached via the northbound Connecticut Turnpike. Uncas, the "last of the Mohicans," is buried there in the Mohegan Indian Burial Ground at the corner of Sachem and Washington Streets. (Variant spellings of Mohegan, such as "Mohican" or "Mohecan," refer to the same Indian tribe.) This was the royal burying ground for the graves of Mohegan sachems and their offspring. Because Uncas had befriended white settlers by leading his Mohegans against other Indian tribes, President Andrew Jackson laid the cornerstone of a granite shaft in Uncas's honor in 1833, and descendants of those settlers completed the monument in 1842.

According to one gravestone in the burial ground, Uncas was not the last of the Mohicans. Though James Fenimore Cooper never mentioned it, Uncas had a son, Sunseeto, who probably died after his father. He is buried nearby. His epitaph reads:

> *Sunseeto*
> *Here lies the body of Sunseeto*
> *Own son to Uncas, grandson to Oneeko*
> *But now they are all dead, I think it is werheegan* [good news].

Before leaving Norwich, you might like to go a few blocks north of the burial grounds to the intersection of Washington Street and Arnold Place. In a house on Arnold Place, Benedict Arnold was born.

Lebanon is northwest of Norwich on Route 87. In Liberty Hill Cemetery, the headstone above the grave of Capt. S. L. Gray proclaims that he "died on board ship James Murray near the island of Guam, March 24, 1865." He wasn't buried until a year later, when his body arrived in Lebanon—encased in a sealed cask of rum! (You might say he arrived home in good spirits.) He was still in the keg when buried. Legend has it that Captain Gray died during a sea battle with a famous Confederate raider, the *Shenandoah*. His wife, who occasionally sailed with him during long sea voyages, took command of the ship, eluded the *Shenandoah*, and reached Guam on March 24. Refusing to bury her husband in the Pacific, Mrs. Gray ordered a large barrel of rum to be opened, had her husband's body immersed within it, and had the cask tightly sealed again for its long journey home.

Not all of this is true. The captain's ship was actually the *James L. Maury*, and it sailed from New Bedford under his command on June 1, 1864, bound for the Pacific whaling grounds and the Bering Sea. According to the ship's log, Captain Gray did die aboard ship, not in battle but while the ship was actually in Guam. Captain Gray died after a two-day illness; in a letter Mrs. Gray attributed his death to "inflammation of the bowels." The circumstances of his burial are not known for sure.

North of Lebanon, the Natchaug State Forest is up in the northeast corner of the state alongside Route 198. To locate the forest from the intersection of U.S. 44 and Route 198, head south on 198, take the first left, then the next left. Look for a brown post next to mailboxes at a right turn. A short distance beyond on the right is the small Nathaniel Lyon Memorial Park. An old stone chimney about ten feet square is all that remains of Nathaniel Lyon's birthplace. Nathaniel Lyon is a little-known hero of the Civil War. He was the first general to be killed in that struggle and may be the world's only military hero whose memory is marked by a stone chimney. General Lyon died in battle at Wilson's Creek in Missouri

Nathaniel Lyon Memorial

on August 10, 1861, having had two horses shot from under him first. He lost that battle, but in doing so, he saved Missouri for the Union. With 4,500 Union soldiers, Lyon adopted an unusual battle tactic by splitting his small force to attack a Confederate Army of 11,600. He nearly succeeded, but when the attack failed and the Union troops fled, the Confederates were so badly disorganized they were unable to pursue. General Lyon's aggressive operations kept Missouri in the Union. In Saint Louis, Missouri, a school was named for him and two equestrian statues erected in his honor. A reported fifteen thousand persons attended his funeral in Eastford, Connecticut. He is buried nearby in the Phoenixville Cemetery.

Woodstock is a short side trip north of Phoenixville on Route 198. At number 1728 on Route 198 is the Photomobile Model Museum, which contains a unique collection of model boats, cars, trains, planes, and hovercraft—all of them powered by solar energy. Weather permitting, visitors can ride in a full scale solar-powered golf cart or canoe. Videotapes, slide shows, and still photos explain how solar energy works. An unusual feature is the working model of a MAGLEV train, one that is moved by "magnetic levitation." MAGLEV is a technique in which a vehicle on a rail is moved by using magnetic fields created by magnets at the bottom of the train and beneath the track. The wheels never touch the guiding rails, so the ride is smooth and swift. This transportation technology is already being used in Japan and Germany. The superspeed MAGLEV Transrapid connecting Hamburg with Berlin covers 180 miles in less than an hour and can go as fast as three hundred miles per hour.

A short distance west of the museum is I-84. To reach Tolland, go south on I-84 to Exit 68. Grant Hill Road, near the exit, leads to Metcalf Road. At 160 Metcalf Road is the Daniel Benton Homestead, popularly believed to be haunted by the tragedy of two lovers, buried separately on the west lawn with a giant sycamore tree between them. Daniel Benton had lost one son in the French and Indian Wars and three of his grandsons were captured by the British during the Revolutionary War. One of them, Elisha, contracted smallpox while on a British prison ship. Exchanged and sent home, he was a danger to anyone who came in contact with him. Jemima Barrows volunteered to take care of Elisha, who had hoped to marry her in spite of his family's earlier objection to her lower social status. The dying soldier and his beloved were quarantined inside two adjacent rooms during his few remaining weeks. After his death, Elisha's body was removed through a window to avoid further contamination within the household. Having contracted the disease herself, Jemima lived only a short time longer. Since side-by-side burial was traditionally reserved for husband and wife, a road once divided their graves, but a stone marker with a plaque now stands between them next to the tree shading both. How haunted is the Benton Homestead? A girl dressed as a bride is seen inside the house and heard sobbing. A photographer outside the house finds that neither of his two cameras will work. A visiting psychic detects the presence of a man wearing a Revolutionary War uniform. You be the judge.

Winsted is in the opposite corner of the state on Route 8 north of Torrington. You can ask the people at the local newspaper to show you their photograph of Louis T. Stone. Early in this century, roadside signboards greeted visitors by announcing that Winsted had been put on the map by stories Louis Stone wrote for newspapers. A plaque on the building of the Winsted *Evening Citizen* honored him and a bridge over Sucker Brook was named for him. Back in 1895, the large metropolitan dailies were not interested in buying small-town stories submitted by cub reporter Stone. Needing money, Stone decided to produce news that editors couldn't resist. His fictitious account of a wild man roaming loose in the Connecticut woods got an immediate editorial reaction. Among many other tales that news-hungry metropolitan editors scrambled to get and that were quite often reported as true stories, Stone followed up with news items about a tree on which baked apples grew; a farmer who plucked his hens for market with a vacuum cleaner; a rattlesnake that exploded when it bit into a tire; a hen that laid a red, white, and blue egg on July 4; a cat with a harelip who could whistle "Yankee Doodle"; a man who painted a spider on his bald head to keep flies away; and a cow so modest it kicked over the pail when a man would try to milk her. Sadly, the only existing memento of the "Winsted Liar"—the man who put the town on the map—is the photograph hanging on an inside wall of the local newspaper office.

On your way south toward Waterbury, detour a few miles west on U.S. 202 to Litchfield. Ethan Allen was born there on Old South Road and Harriet Beecher Stowe was born on North Street. Those birth facts pale beside the cemetery epitaph of

> *Mrs. Mary, wife of Deacon John Buel, Esq. She died Nov. 4, 1768, aged 90—having had 13 children, 101 Grand-children, 247 Grate-Grand-Children, and 49 Grate-Grate-Grand-Children; total 410. Three Hundred and Thirty Six Survived her.*

Waterbury is south on Route 8, but before you reach it, stop at the Mattatuck State Forest and ask about the "Leather Man's cave," so called because its occasional inhabitant was clad entirely in leather. This strange character appeared in the early 1860s and continued for twenty-seven years to walk along a set route passing through western Connecticut and eastern New York. From his crazy cap to his high moccasins, his clothing was a well-ventilated patchwork made up of odd pieces of leather cut from the tops of high, old-fashioned boots and laced awkwardly together with wide thongs. In the winter he wore leather mittens. He shouldered a leather bag containing his worldly goods. Traveling at a constant pace, the Leather Man walked the same 366-mile circuit regularly every thirty-four days, 240 miles in Connecticut and 126 in New York. His starting point was Harwinton, Connecticut, and if he was delayed anywhere in carrying out his schedule, he would cut short the last part so he could get back to Harwinton and start a new trip on time. At the end of each day, he slept in a lean-to or a cave (the cave in Mattatuck State Forest was one), but he never slept in a building. Neither a peddler nor a beggar, he was never known to smile and seldom uttered a word, but he accepted food, tobacco, and small change from those who were friendly enough to offer it. He was found dead in a cave near Mount Pleasant,

New York, on March 24, 1889. No one ever knew who the Leather Man really was, but children immortalized him in a nursery rhyme:

> *One misty, moisty morning when cloudy was the weather,*
> *I chanced to meet an old man clothed all in leather.*

Travelers in the Waterbury area on I-84 near Exit 22 can't help but notice a large wooden cross on a high hill close to the road. It marks the location of "Holy Land," a miniature replica of Jerusalem and Bethlehem, constructed on a terraced hilltop at the end of Fuller Street and overlooking the city. A stone cave represents the stable in which Christ was born. Herod's palace is there, as well as a small sphinx and pyramid, a slab dedicated to the Reverend Martin Luther King, and, on a small rise, three crosses with the figure of Christ on the center one. Most of the holy buildings, unseen from the road, are less than two feet high and clumsily constructed, but viewed from the winding paths surrounding them, they are an impressive sight. Close up, it's apparent that time and vandals have been at work. Years ago Holy Land was a featured item on the official state maps, but today, it's no longer advertised as a public attraction. Now owned by the Queen of Apostles Convent (which accepts donations to their Holy Land Fund), there seems to be no objection to visitors continuing to view this unique religious monument.

Traveling west on I-84 from Waterbury toward New York, Southbury is at Exit 15. About two and a half miles south of that town on Russian Village Road is Churaevka, a small village started in 1923 by Count Ilya Tolstoy, grandson of the famous Russian writer, and Grebenshchikoff, a novelist and lecturer. The thirty-five landowners who settled there were members of the Imperial Army before the Russian Revolution. Intended as a quiet retreat for displaced White Russians, the Russian dachas (simply constructed summer homes set on large, open lawns) have gradually been transformed into contemporary-style residences. Russian art adorns the long row of postboxes, but names like Moore have now joined Romanoff and Alexandrow. The tiny Ukranian church (or chapel) with its dome and colorful facade is visible on the left as you enter the village, and is the only obvious remnant of the Russian influence.

If you don't mind another brief side trip, head for the Quaker Farm Cemetery on Route 188 southeast from Southbury. Capt. Zachariah Hawkins, a ninety-year-old who died in 1806, is buried there. According to his epitaph, "He had 14 children, who all survived him, 2 grand-children, & 95 great-grand-children." (From only two grandchildren?)

One of the minor mysteries of the Revolutionary War is buried with Squire William Heron in the cemetery beside the Christ Episcopal Church in Redding (south of Danbury on Route 101). Heron had been an active patriot and a trusted friend of Samuel Parsons, a general in the Continental army. Late in August 1780 he told Parsons he had to go to New York to collect a debt. Parsons sent Heron to Benedict Arnold for the necessary pass. After a lengthy wait, Arnold gave Heron the pass along with a letter to be delivered in New York to a "John Anderson." Heron was suspicious about the secrecy involved with delivery, but he agreed. Once in New York, however, Heron contacted the British, made an agreement with them, and became a British spy for the rest of the war.

Strangely, however, he did not produce the suspicious letter Arnold gave him. Instead he gave it to his patriot friend Parsons when he returned to Redding. Parsons read it as simply a commercial communication and did not turn it over to General Washington until after Arnold's treachery was discovered. "John Anderson" was really Maj. John Andre. Had Heron delivered the letter to New York, perhaps new arrangements might have allowed Arnold's treachery to go undiscovered. Had Parsons been suspicious when he read the letter, Arnold's treachery might have been discovered earlier. The real mystery is why Heron failed to turn the letter over to the British after he agreed to become a spy. To date, no one seems to have the answer.

There are two oddities about Ridgefield, a charming town west of Redding on Route 35, which incidentally has one of the most beautiful rural main streets in America. During his patriotic period, Benedict Arnold became a hero in Ridgefield. A cannonball embedded in Keeler Tavern (and still visible in that wall) attests to the battle and Arnold's heroism. On April 26, 1777, Arnold was at home in New Haven when he learned that the British were marching on Danbury to fire the ammunition and supply depots there. The British then moved to Ridgefield to burn a military warehouse. Arnold had gathered four hundred men, who dug trenches and built breastworks to block the British. Outnumbered five to one, they repulsed three British charges and inflicted a heavy toll, killing seventy British before the tide of battle turned. Arnold was the last to retreat. As he wheeled his horse, a British volley put nine bullets into his steed and Arnold fell, pinned under the horse. Seeing this, the Americans ran, leaving Arnold to face the enemy alone. As a redcoat soldier charged him, shouting, "Surrender," Arnold yanked free. "Not yet!" he cried, then killed the soldier, vaulted a fence, scrambled into a swamp, and escaped. On May 2, an embarrassed Congress that had continually denied promotion to him, learned of Arnold's bravery and finally promoted him to major general.

The second oddity lies in the aftermath of that battle. Many patriots really thought of themselves as abused Englishmen and felt an uncomfortable sympathy for the soldiers sent to fight them. A plaque commemorating the event says that the eight patriots who died "were laid in this ground, Companied by Sixteen British Soldiers, Living their enemies, Dying, their guests." A sensitive and gracious gesture from a village that had been an unwilling battleground.

Two documents have helped create our public image of Connecticut. When it was still the Hartford colony, it adopted the Fundamental Orders for governing the colony. That document may be the world's first written constitution and is often cited as the basis for the U.S. Constitution, another reason why "Constitution State" is printed on the Connecticut license plates. For years, however, Connecticut has suffered under the popular belief that a second set of rules governed social behavior within the state. These were the notorious blue laws, usually thought of as a rigid code of conduct enforced against a reluctant public. Among them:

No one shall cross a river but with an authorized ferryman.
No woman shall kiss her child on the Sabbath or fasting day.

Married persons must live together or be imprisoned.
No one shall run on the Sabbath day or walk in his garden.

These laws, and others like them, were listed by the Reverend Samuel A. Peters in his *General History of Connecticut by a Gentleman of the Province*, published in London in 1781. He was a loyalist clergyman who had fled the colonies seven years earlier. His compilation of anti-American exaggerations and inaccuracies reflected his animosity.

Now it so happens that the legal records of Connecticut are unusually complete and, under further scrutiny, these blue laws seemed to be missing. A detailed search showed that about half of the blue laws listed by Peters did exist in New Haven, a few more existed in New England colonies outside of Connecticut, nine more were erroneous, and eight were completely spurious. Actually, blue laws had existed in the colonies since 1619, when Virginia required men to dress according to their rank and taxed any excess in that dress code. In 1656 Captain Kemble of Boston spent two hours in stocks for "his lewd and unseemly behavior." Having just returned from a three-year voyage, he was judged guilty of kissing his wife publicly on Sunday. So Peters was not solely to blame. Twenty-eight of his "laws" were quoted from *The History of New England*, by Daniel Neal, published in London in 1747. Still, Connecticut continues to suffer today under the old adage, "History doesn't repeat itself. It's the historians, repeating what earlier historians have said."

Come to think of it, that's how this book got written.

ACKNOWLEDGMENTS

I am deeply in debt to many persons without whose help and encouragement this book would never have been written. Albert LaFarge, my editor, gently and tactfully brought order out of my verbal chaos. My agent, Sandra Taylor, not only found a publisher but patiently bore the burdens imposed on her by a novice author, while Barbara Smullen's enthusiasm graced her obvious artistic talent; it was Meade Cadot who put me in touch with both of them. My son, Geoffrey, and friends like Dot Grim (who sacrificed part of a golfing occasion) conducted field research and took photographs. Denny, my wife, handled logistics, took photographs to provide details for the illustrations, kept records, found places where we could enjoy our mid-morning snack by the side of the road, and steered me in the right direction. Suggestions came from many helpful sources. Left unlisted but certainly remembered are all of the busy people who took enough time to answer my inquiries with personal memories, copies of local documents and newsclips, and ideas for my consideration. I am very grateful to all of you.

INDEX OF PLACE NAMES